Careers
With
Animals

Exploring Occupations Involving
Dogs, Horses, Cats,
Birds, Wildlife, and Exotics

Ellen Shenk

D1366704

STACKPOLE
BOOKS

0 11557 02962 8

Published by
STACKPOLE BOOKS
5067 Ritter Road
Mechanicsburg, PA 17055
www.stackpolebooks.com

Printed in the United States of America

10 9 8 7 6 5 4 3 2 1

First edition

Cover photograph by Skip Noll/Getty Images
Cover design by Caroline Stover

Library of Congress Cataloging-in-Publication Data

Shenk, Ellen.
   Careers with animals : exploring occupations involving dogs, horses, cats, birds, wildlife, and exotics / Ellen Shenk.
     p. cm.
  Includes bibliographical references and index.
   ISBN 0-8117-2962-1
  1. Animal specialists—Vocational guidance—United States. 2. Animal specialists—Vocational guidance—Canada. I. Title.

SF80.S48 2005
636'.0023—dc22
2004027273

Contents

Acknowledgments

In the process of researching, organizing, and writing the book I had help from a great many people. Adequately thanking everyone will be impossible but I need to try. To begin with, I thank my friends and family, who provided support and encouragement through the long months of researching, writing, and decision-making, especially Philip, who took me to the wild cat sanctuary and helped me deal with my innate aversion to reptiles at the reptile zoo. My editors at Stackpole provided invaluable help in both the writing and the editing. Mark Allison gave suggestions and feedback at times when I needed both, in addition to editing; Chris Chappell's editing and attention to production details eased the final steps in bringing the book to publication. Both were extremely capable and very pleasant to deal with.

Although a great deal of the information for the book came from the Internet, books, and magazine articles, experts in various fields and organizations were extremely helpful in sharing their knowledge and in reading and critiquing portions of the book. In the process these strangers became friends. It is virtually impossible to name them all. Although they include the individuals profiled in the book, many other people generously shared their knowledge. I am very grateful for their help.

Ellen Shenk

Introduction

Animals are such agreeable friends—they ask
no questions, they pass no criticism.
George Eliot, "Mr. Filfil's Love-Story"

Humans have an age-old relationship with animals. Exactly when the relationship changed from one of antagonism and conflict to one of companionship and cooperation, at least with some species of animals, is not known. For thousands of years, however, the human-animal relationship has been an important force in the survival of our species. The fascination that humans have with animals is shown in the many books about animals and the abundance of quotes dealing with animals sprinkled throughout literature.

As individuals look for satisfying and fulfilling work, career experts suggest that they should carefully factor into this search their own personal interests. A love of animals is one such interest that is shared by many people.

This book examines a wide spectrum of work that relates to animals. Its premise, as with much career literature, is that before people invest a great deal of time and money to prepare for any specific type of work, they should be as certain as possible that this is the kind of work they should be doing. Knowledge and experience are key to this certainty.

THE KNOWLEDGE FACTOR

To aid individuals in gaining knowledge, this book provides information on various types of work with animals. Because the subject is quite broad, this information can only serve as an introduction. It is up to individuals to pinpoint their interests more precisely. The resource listing in each chapter can be a starting point for further exploration of job opportunities in a specific field.

A good way to learn about kinds of work is to talk to the experts—the people doing that work. Ask for details about the work and its positive and negative aspects. In this research, it is important to talk to more than one person and also to talk with people in different professional settings (for example, a rural veterinarian who works alone as well as one who belongs to a suburban group practice). The profiles included in this book deal with a variety of types of work and provide a starting point in this research.

THE EXPERIENCE FACTOR

It's equally helpful to get actual experience in work that appears interesting. You can get hands-on experience with animals through volunteer work, part-time or summer jobs, and internships that involve animals. One value of actual work experience is that it helps you discover the strength of your passion for a given animal or kind of work. If you find that your passion is not strong enough to carry you through the negative aspects of a job, you will have saved the expenses of education for this career. On the other hand, working in a specific field may confirm that this is the right work for you. Additionally, you may discover allergies that would make certain jobs difficult or other factors that eliminate possible careers. These factors may not be discovered short of doing the actual work. Other benefits include the experience, inside knowledge, and contacts gained in volunteer, part-time, or summer work; these can be helpful in getting a full-time job at a later date.

It is wise to get broad experience with different types of jobs and different types of animals. You may be initially interested in one type of animal but change your mind as you experience work with another.

OTHER CONSIDERATIONS

As you evaluate a career with animals, be sure to consider all the factors about this type of work. For one, many animal-related careers are not high-paying; some people think of them as more of a "lifestyle choice" than a nine-to-five job. Additionally, many of these job possibilities do not provide a life-sustaining income but are part-time, weekend, or volunteer work.

You may realize, after exploring work possibilities, that the work that really appeals to you would not be able to support you financially. Many people have found a satisfying life by doing one type of work for financial support and using weekends and other free time to work part-time with animals. Others have pulled several part-time jobs together to create a satisfying and financially sound lifestyle. So if earning a large sum of money is very important to you, your work with animals may need to be volunteer or part-time.

Another factor of work with animals is that many of these jobs are physically difficult. Personal fitness is essential in some of the work. An important personality trait is patience. Some things—training animals, waiting to get just the right picture, or teaching horse riding— simply cannot be hurried on the job.

When exploring jobs with animals, the actual name given to a job is not as important as its content—the tasks and responsibilities that it entails. Jobs for herpetologists or ornithologists, for example, will vary tremendously in actual content. Although the name will be the first thing that attracts you to a job, read the description of the job carefully to ensure that it involves the actual work that interests you.

CATEGORIES OF WORK WITH ANIMALS

Although this book is primarily organized by animal type, careers with animals can also be divided by job content into seven categories. These categories are listed below, along with brief descriptions of the possibilities available in each.

Breeding and Raising Animals

Many animals are bred as part of a very deliberate and careful process. Zoo breeding programs, for example, work to continue species threatened with extinction. Some animals, such as rats, are bred to have certain traits for research purposes. Police horses may be bred for personality characteristics, such as temperament. For other animals the process may be more haphazard. Pigs, elk, deer, and other animals are simply raised for food, and sometimes for on-ranch hunting, and do not need to be as carefully bred.

Training Animals

Animals are trained for many different reasons. Horses are trained to ride, to show, and to race. Personal assistance animals are trained to help people who are hearing-impaired, have an illness with seizures such as epilepsy, or are mobility-impaired. Dogs are trained for obedience, for shows, and for competitions such as herding. Some animals are trained to do tricks for circuses or aquatic shows while others are trained for roles in movies or television shows. Animals kept in captivity are trained in what are known as husbandry behaviors to make their care easier and less stressful.

Caring for Animals
Much of the work in caring for animals is performed by veterinarians and veterinary assistants, but specialized care such as massage, acupuncture, and other kinds of treatment are becoming increasingly common. Behaviorists deal with animal behaviors that present problems to humans. Other types of work that involve caring for animals include animal sitting and walking, pet grooming, shelter work, and boarding kennel operation.

Preserving Animals
Much of the work in the category of preserving animals is related to species and environmental concerns. People in this field may work at wildlife preserves or as wildlife rehabilitators, wildlife biologists, marine biologists, and fish and game officers. Zoo staff at all skill levels fall into this category, as do people who work at animal refuges or sanctuaries. Some of this work aims to educate the public about the need to preserve different species and animal habitats.

Working with Animals
Some people work with animals in the course of an occupation that is otherwise not animal-related. These include police who work with K-9 units and mounted police, such as the Royal Canadian Mounted Police, who use horses for transportation. People who show and judge animals fall into this category, as do racehorse jockeys and harness racers.

Harvesting Animals or Animal Products
Animal products that are harvested today include honey, milk, feathers or down, and wool. Raising animals for meat falls into this category, as does work with fisheries and in aquaculture.

Observing Animals

Photographers and animal artists observe domestic and wild animals, often for long periods at a time. Other observers portray animals in books, magazines, and films.

HOW TO USE THIS BOOK

The book is organized around animal types, with the exception of Chapter 10, which covers medicine and therapy for animals. Where similar work is described in several different chapters, it has been cross-referenced to assist readers in finding related information elsewhere in the book. Note that pay rates and certain other information are simply a guide to what is average for a given job. Pay varies tremendously from location to location and from employer to employer and is also dependent on the state of the economy.

A book of this size cannot possibly provide every last bit of information about work with animals. It is intended to help you narrow down your choices and focus on work that you believe will interest you. Then the real work begins—individual research is an essential part of the career search, and the Resources sections in each chapter are given to help you begin your search for additional, more detailed information.

Good luck!

Chapter 1

Choosing Your Career

*Successful careers seldom happen by chance. With very
few exceptions, people who really get what they want in a
career do so because they define clear objectives, develop
plans and schedules for achieving their objectives, assume
personal responsibility for implementing and following
these plans, monitor their progress regularly, improve
their plans when they aren't getting the desired results,
and persevere in the face of frequent setbacks until their
objects are achieved.*

Nicholas Weiler, *Reality and Career Planning*

People choose careers in various ways. Some simply accept any
position that is available and looks interesting. Others take a job
because they know someone who does that type of work or works for
the same organization. Still others take time for some self-assessment
to discover who they really are and what they can and want to do.
They then do research to learn what kinds of careers fit the type of person they are.

The fact that you have picked up this book probably means that
you fall into this last category. Because many careers require extensive
training, it is wise to research carefully before making your choice.
Even if you are quite certain which career you wish to enter, take a little
time to be sure you are headed in the best possible direction for the
unique person you are.

One of the first steps in choosing a career is to complete a personal
inventory. This will help you better define your unique characteristics
and what you want to do. Important components are your interests,
skills, and values.

You chose to read this book because work with animals is important
to you. What you need to decide is what role animals should play
in your career. Do you want to work directly with animals, deal with a

subject matter that relates to animals, work for an organization that is concerned with animals, or a combination of these? Consider these options as you continue to read this book.

INTERESTS

Your interests are one key factor in career decision-making. It is important to select a field in which you will be working with issues, content, subject matter, or animals that you care about. It is much more pleasant to spend thirty-five to forty or more hours a week doing work that greatly interests you than something that bores you. Being aware of your interests can help you identify potential work environments and employers.

As you work through the following exercises picking out your skills and values, use interest as a criterion to keep or eliminate items from your list. For example, although you may be skilled at drawing, you may not like to do it. Picking a career that uses a skill, however well developed, that doesn't interest you would be counterproductive—you would not really enjoy that career.

SKILLS

When you examine different careers, it's important to know whether your skills match those required for that career. If you have completed a skills inventory, you will be able to decide whether a particular career is a good fit for you.

A skill is generally defined as "something you do well." Some of your skills may come to mind immediately. But because we aren't always tuned in to the things we do well, it is a good idea to spend some time assessing your skills.

The following list contains some of the skills you should consider. As you read through these skills, write down those that apply to you. Consider skills you have used in clubs, extracurricular activities, or hobbies, as well as on part-time or volunteer jobs or in school.

administer	coordinate	evaluate
analyze	counsel	explain
arrange	create	formulate
assemble	delegate	fund-raise
build	design	guide
calculate	dramatize	interpret
coach	edit	interview

investigate	persuade	sell
keep records	plan	sketch
listen	predict	speak publicly
manage	print	supervise
measure	promote	talk
mediate	question	teach
negotiate	recruit	translate
observe	repair	troubleshoot
organize	research	write

This list is by no means exhaustive; you will want to add other skills that occur to you. Also, as you write down your skills, it's helpful to add an example of a situation when you used each one. For example, you might note under "keep records" that as a 4-H club treasurer for three years, you kept accurate records of the membership dues paid and the results of special sales projects.

VALUES

Also vital to consider when making a career choice are your values—those things that are most important to you. Values provide satisfaction and add purpose and fulfillment to life. Often people do not realize that their values don't match those of their chosen profession until they are well into a career. Figuring out this part of the career match before you make other choices can help you avoid problems later on.

Read the following list and write down the values that are important to you.

achievement	perform important roles and be involved in momentous endeavors
autonomy	be free to work with little supervision and set your own schedule and priorities
distinction	be well known, be seen as successful, and have recognition and status in your chosen field
expertise	become a respected and trusted expert in your field
friendship	like and be liked by the people with whom you work
leadership	be an influential and respected leader
location	be able to live and work in the places you choose
pleasure	find enjoyment and have fun doing your work

power	be able to approve or disapprove different courses of action, make assignments, and control allocations and outcomes
security	obtain a secure and stable position
self-realization	do work that is challenging and allows you to fully develop your talents
service	help people in need and contribute to the satisfaction of others
wealth	earn a great deal of money so that you can be financially independent

Jot down any other values that are important to you. At this stage of the decision-making process, it is helpful to write down as much information about yourself as possible.

TEMPERAMENT AND PERSONAL QUALITIES

Take a few moments to examine your personality and temperament. Are you outgoing, patient, reflective, conscientious, or responsible? Which are your traits that you like best and would like to use on the job? Write these down, giving examples. You should resist the temptation to select personal qualities that you value, rather than ones that you actually possess.

SUMMER, PART-TIME, AND VOLUNTEER WORK

Knowing your interests, skills, values, and personal qualities will help you make a better match as you investigate the careers in this book. Another aid in deciding on a career is to actually do the type of work that interests you. Many types of work with animals are available on a summer, part-time, or volunteer basis. A careful search can land you a summer or short-term job in the type of setting you believe best matches your needs and desires.

You may also want to check into volunteer work related to the field you're considering. Many communities have agencies that seek to match volunteers with jobs, and these can help you in your search. With a little persistence, however, you should be able to arrange your own volunteer position. Many organizations are under-funded and even those with no cash-flow problems may be quite happy to have a volunteer helping out.

Working in the setting of the type of work that interests you—or at least in one that is similar—can help you decide whether you really want to do that work. And the contacts you make in your summer, part-time, or volunteer work can be invaluable to you later when you actually begin your job search.

ADDITIONAL CAREER-SEARCH RESOURCES

At this point you may not yet be certain about the exact career that appeals to you and want to do some additional searching. Don't despair! Sometimes it simply takes a while to settle on a career. Doing some background research before you spend a lot of time and money preparing for a particular career is very worthwhile. Help is as close as your public library, bookstore, telephone, or Internet access point.

You may decide that you want a career counselor to help you identify your interests, skills, and values; locate resources to explore different career options; or prepare for the job search. A career counselor can help you by providing an objective eye; it is often difficult to see yourself clearly. Counselors are also helpful in guiding you through the self-evaluation process if you get stuck.

Career counselors can be located fairly easily. One place to look is at nearby colleges and universities, most of which offer career counseling to their students. Many extend free use of this service to their graduates, and some also serve the public, although usually for a fee. Nonprofit organizations, government agencies, and employment centers also offer career counseling, usually at little or no cost.

Private career counselors can be quite good—although the cost will be higher than most other counseling sources—and many people find this type of counseling the most helpful. These counselors can be located in the yellow pages or through friends and relatives.

Before you invest too much time or money, make certain that the counselor will be helpful to you. Arrange for a fifteen-minute free visit to see whether you feel comfortable with him or her. A good personality match is important in counseling. Also find out whether the counselor is a Nationally Certified Career Counselor, shown by the acronym NCCC following his or her name. This certification indicates professional recognition, a commitment to continuing education, successful completion of two national exams, recommendations from the field, and supervised experience.

You may also choose to consult one of the excellent books that give in-depth assistance in making career decisions. The books recommended here should be available in libraries or bookstores. You may also locate books not on this list that are very helpful to you. Before you purchase a book, browse through it to ensure that you will find it useful.

USING THE INTERNET

The Internet can also provide assistance in locating a career. Many career counseling services are available online, but most charge a fee. For this reason, especially, it is important to take some care in selecting a service. The background, experience, and expertise of the counselor with whom you would be dealing are essential pieces of information. You should also determine the amount of assistance you can actually gain from a service. For example, does this service only help in self-assessment for choosing a career, or does it also provide help in the nitty-gritty of finding a job: preparing strategies for the job search, writing a resume, locating job possibilities, and preparing for an interview? You will also want to evaluate carefully the charges for the service to determine whether you will be getting your money's worth.

For more information about using the Internet in your job search, see Chapter 11. Be sure to check the Resources listing at the end of that chapter as well.

RESOURCES

Bolles, Richard Nelson. *What Color Is Your Parachute? A Practical Manual for Job-Hunters & Career Changers.* Berkeley, Calif.: Ten Speed Press, updated annually.

Gilman, Cheryl. *Doing Work You Love.* Lincolnwood, Ill.: Contemporary Books, 1997.

Kennedy, Joyce Lain and Darryl Laramore. *Joyce Lain Kennedy's Career Book, 3rd ed.* Lincolnwood, Ill.: VGM, 1997.

Kipps, Harriet Clyde, ed. *Volunteer America: A Comprehensive National Guide to Opportunities for Service, Training, and Work Experience, 4th ed.* Chicago: Ferguson Publishing Company, 1997.

Krannich, Ronald L., and Caryl Krannich. *Discover the Best Jobs for You, 4th ed.* Manassas, Va.: Impact Publications, 2004.

———. *Change Your Job, Change Your Life: Careering and Re-Careering in the New Boom/Bust Economy, 8th ed.* Manassas, Va.: Impact Publications, 2004.

Lore, Nicholas. *The Pathfinder: How to Choose or Change Your Career for a Lifetime of Satisfaction or Success.* New York: Simon & Schuster Inc., A Fireside Book, 1998.

Taylor, Jeff with Doug Hardy. *Monster Careers: How to Land the Job of Your Life.* London: Penguin Books, 2004.

Tieger, Paul D. and Barbara Barron-Tieger. *Do What You Are: Discover the Perfect Career for You Through the Secrets of Personality Type.* Boston: Little, Brown and Company, 2001.

A few helpful websites:

What Color Is Your Parachute?, electronic edition (http://www.jobhuntersbible.com/).

The Career Interests Game at the University of Missouri (career.missouri.edu) is based on the Holland system, which classifies personality types and work environments into six groups: realistic, investigative, artistic, social, enterprising, and conventional.

At http://campus.monster.com/ you can get a great variety of career information by selecting different options from the opening page.

America's Career InfoNet 2004 (http://www.acinet.org/acinet/) has extensive career-related information.

Quintessential Careers (http://www.quintcareers.com) contains varied information about careers and about the job search as well as links to additional data.

Dr. Randal Hansen, Career Coach, provides a huge range of helpful free resources and various levels of pay for coaching at http://www.careerdoctor.org.

Chapter 2

Cats, Dogs, and Other Small Pets

There is no domestic animal which has so radically altered its whole way of living, indeed its whole sphere of interests, that has become domestic in so true a sense as the dog: and there is no animal that, in the course of its century-old association with man, has altered so little as the cat.

Konrad Lorenz, *Man Meets Dog*

According to statistics taken in 2000 and 2001 by the American Pet Products Manufacturers Association, there are approximately 73 million owned cats and 68 million owned dogs in the United States. Considering this, it is logical that many types of work involve these animals in some way. A few are full-time jobs. Others are part-time and must be done in tandem with other work to provide a living. And some are simply volunteer jobs that bring personal satisfaction to the individuals who pursue them.

In this chapter we look at the various jobs that involve cats, dogs, and other small pets, including positions that are available at cat and dog shows. While cats and dogs dominate most of the chapter, it's important to remember that many other small, and sometimes exotic, animals are also sold as pets. Rabbits, ferrets, mice, and hamsters are a few popular examples. (It is estimated that the United States alone has about six million pet ferrets.) Some of the more unusual animals that are sold include sugar gliders, African pygmy hedgehogs, ferrets, black-eyed white prairie dogs, rhesus macaques, and coatimundi. The majority of jobs with such animals can be found in the breeding field. Although some of these animals are not well known, additional information is as close as the library, Internet, bookstore, or pet store. *Critters USA* is an annual publication that deals with these small animals.

Jobs with small animals often entail hard work and minimal pay. Breeding, for instance, is a time-consuming, detail-oriented process that pays very little—rarely enough to earn a good income. It is possible, however, to earn a reasonable income by pursuing several different types of work relating to animals, or by doing another type of work entirely in addition to breeding. People who are interested in working with small animals have to be driven by a passion for the work and must be prepared to diversify their income instead of depending on any one of these jobs.

Because there are so many variables in this work, including the need for additional income and pay differences according to location, it is sometimes impossible to give exact salary information. People interested in the jobs in this chapter will want to conduct further research and contact experienced individuals to learn more about income and other variables.

SMALL ANIMAL BREEDER

Salary Range: A breeder's net annual income is low to non-existent. As a rule of thumb, in a typical litter of five puppies the sale of three puppies will cover the stud fee, the mother's extra care and feeding, and assorted costs for registering and maintaining the litter. For profit this leaves the sale of two puppies, with an average price of $1,000 to $1,200 per puppy. The total costs for a litter of cats (not including maintenance costs of the adult breeding cats) average about $1,400; the income from selling the litter is about the same. The estimates for both dogs and cats do not factor in unexpected costs, such as the expense of a cesarean section during birth.

Educational Requirements: There are no specific educational requirements for breeders. The most successful breeders have a good knowledge of genetics and canine/feline anatomy, both in general and breed-specific terms. This comes from years of personal study, attending courses and seminars, and seeking out mentors in the field.

Employment Outlook: The public's desire for dogs with reproducible and consistent traits and appearance will ensure that dedicated breeders always remain on the scene. Similarly, there continues to be a demand for pure-bred cats, even those of pet quality.

The majority of breeders work with either cats or dogs. Whether a breeder is working with his or her own animals or those of a customer, there are various reasons to breed. Some people want to improve the bloodline of an animal that they already own to get offspring that meet the standards of that breed. Others want to breed champion animals from an already established pedigree. And some individuals do it as a scientific way of improving a breed, emphasizing some of the recognized traits for that breed and de-emphasizing others—for example, breeding Siamese cats to be more substantial than the extremely thin Siamese that has been so popular for some years. Prospective breeders must evaluate their motives carefully before they begin. The best reasons to breed cats or dogs are that you love the animals (especially the breed you've chosen) and you want to spend more time with them and breed as close to the breed standard as possible.

Breeding is much more complex than buying purebred animals and getting them to reproduce. Would-be breeders must know the standard of the breed of cat or dog to be bred and whether their animal meets this standard. Each breed has different qualities to take into consideration. Some have specific health and genetic considerations, and temperament and performance are different for each breed. Breeders must be able to identify which offspring can be used for breeding ("show quality" animals) and which will be sold to people who will not breed them ("pet quality" animals). Thoughtful planning is essential, as each breeding decision can affect the future of the breed.

Breeding also entails a great many expenses, such as veterinary care (including testing and vaccinations), good-quality food, housing, insurance, property taxes, and advertising, which often involves showing the dogs to gain the champion designation. If breeding is done in hopes of turning a quick profit, the breeder is likely to be disappointed, especially in the first few years.

Breeding is one area in which work can be done with ferrets, rabbits, and other more unusual pets. However, profits may be just as elusive. Julie and Kevin Groninga of West Valley Wuzzles' Ferret Breeding report: "It's been our experience that breeding and raising ferrets is *not* a profitable hobby or means of income. In fact, if the breeder is taking good care of their ferrets, giving them proper medical attention and raising the kits with proper food and such, you will spend far more than you could ever make from adopting and selling the kits. Of course, on the other side of the coin, there are breeders that neglect their ferrets, keep them in horrible conditions, and provide little or no veterinary care. Sure, they may make a little profit, but at what cost to the welfare of the animals?" Persons who want to breed small animals in a way that is kind and thoughtful must keep this in mind.

Lucille Pakalnis, owner of Dunnescroft Kennels in North Gower, Ontario, has bred Irish wolfhounds since 1984. She says, "I was attracted to the breed because of their magnificent physical size and form, place of origin—I am Irish on my mother's side—and ancient heritage. They are living history. They are also a 'natural' breed to raise and show—that is, there is no fancy grooming or ear or tail cropping." Since 1986 Pakalnis has averaged a litter every year or year and a half.

Pakalnis chose to make her breeding enterprise an actual business and registered it as such. "This requires following the rules and regulations of the Canadian Kennel Club and also the provincial guidelines for small business," she says. "When done this way, buyers have the confidence that they are dealing with a professional kennel, and this goes a long way towards setting and maintaining the relationship between us."

Pakalnis, who enjoys breeding, says, "Misfortune does occur, and every breeder has known the disappointment of a breeding that does not produce puppies, or the loss of puppies due to illness or accident. But the joys are handing a puppy over to a tearfully happy buyer who tells you that you have fulfilled a lifelong dream or receiving a letter from another who says your puppy has become the best dog they have ever had. These make all the sleepless nights and emotional roller-coasters worthwhile."

See profile on page 42.

DOG OR CAT TRAINER

Salary Range: $10 to $25 an hour; pay depends on location and type of training.

Educational Requirements: Study of animal behavior or veterinary medicine are helpful; experience working with many different breeds of cats or dogs is essential.

Employment Outlook: The outlook for dog trainers, especially for general obedience classes, is good. Cat trainers face a smaller and more competitive market.

By far, the majority of small animal trainers work with dogs. Whereas cat trainers work primarily on movies and television programs or for pet owners, dog trainers perform a much wider variety of roles, from obedience training to preparing a dog for service of some kind. Most of this section is devoted to dog trainers; information on training cats can be found on page 19.

There are three types of dog trainers: some teach dogs, some teach owners, and some teach both. They work in varied settings, from group classes to individual work with owners who are interested in entering their dogs in competitions, such as obedience or agility. Few dog trainers do this work full-time; many balance other work with training or train dogs on only a part-time basis.

Dog trainers need to be physically fit, patient, goal-oriented, and self-starting. Insight into and understanding of dog behaviors as well as common sense and determination are other important traits. Most of all, they must have a great love of dogs, the ability to bond with them, and the ability to teach them along with the humans who own them.

The most important background for training dogs is hands-on experience. Study of animal behavior is definitely an asset, but nothing is as important as actual experience, which can be gained through work—paid or volunteer—in animal shelters, veterinary offices, pet stores, or a dog-grooming business. After gaining experience in different settings, the next step is to find work assisting an experienced trainer. This kind of informal apprenticeship is essential for understanding the work and learning the best ways to train.

Methods of training dogs are as different as are individual trainers. Teaching a person to train a dog is, therefore, extremely difficult. It is possible to learn how other trainers do their work, but each individual's attitudes, aptitudes, and sensitivities are different. Additionally, each dog is different, and methods that will work with one dog may not work with another. All trainers need to find the methods that will work for them and for the dog being trained. To do this they need to be learning continually, whether they're studying canine attributes and behavior, the structure of dog societies, or the theories about ways that dogs learn and how to train them. In addition to their hands-on experience, prospective trainers can begin this process by training their own dogs, and entering them in obedience trials or shows with assistance as needed from a dog trainer.

Additionally, good books about dog training and behavior are available. Also helpful are courses, seminars, workshops, and conferences that focus on dog training, many of them sponsored by professional organizations in the various fields of training dogs. Prospective trainers should evaluate commercial dog training schools carefully by talking to previous students and learning where they now work.

Professional organizations, which seek to uphold professionalism in the field, are among the best places to learn. Membership in these organizations is especially important for dog trainers, as it allows them to attend conferences and network with other trainers. Most organizations produce helpful newsletters and books as well. Trainers may also choose to pursue certification, which is available through groups such as the National Association of Dog Obedience Instructors and further enhances a trainer's credentials and professional expertise. Another organization that offers certification is the Association of Pet Dog Trainers (APDT). To encourage professionalism, the APDT has a national accredited certification for pet dog trainers. The "CPDT" designation shows that an individual has a basic knowledge of training theory and a minimum number of hours of lead instruction.

A sometimes underrated part of dog training is the ability to work with people. Dog trainers must like and be able to get along with all types of people. They must be able to listen to dog owners and to teach and motivate them, though they will be of various ages and abilities. Dog trainers also may be asked to solve problems between dogs and owners. This can be especially true in obedience training, where owners come to the class because they want an obedient companion or have problems with their dogs that they cannot solve.

The actual work of training dogs and educating owners is not all that dog trainers do. Since many trainers work independently, they need to develop skills in operating and organizing a business, and they must be disciplined in their time commitments. They also need to market their services, and here creativity, careful planning, and public speaking skills can come in handy. Dog trainers who do not have their own business may work with pet-related businesses such as pet stores, veterinarians, groomers, and animal shelters. City or county recreation departments, 4-H clubs, or other community groups may also hire some trainers.

In a recent survey, the APDT learned that more than eighty-five percent of their members trained dogs part-time. Many part-time trainers have income from other work that is not even dog-related, whereas others make additional money from grooming services, boarding kennels, or doggie daycare.

Dogs are trained for many different uses. The large majority of dog trainers train companion dogs for obedience—to follow the orders of their owners. Some dogs are trained to show and to be judged on their appearance and conformation. Dogs also are trained to be service dogs, assisting people with vision problems or other physical impairments in their daily activities. Some dogs are trained to actually help in various kinds of therapy. Search-and-rescue dogs, which assist in finding disaster victims, also need training, although most commonly the owners, who are also their handlers, train their own dogs for work in this difficult field.

Obedience Training for Dogs. Dog obedience trainers usually work as freelancers or in private obedience schools. The main reason to train dogs for obedience is to add to the pleasure and ease of having them as companions. When dogs are trained to walk on a leash, outdoor excursions become easier and more pleasant for owner and pet alike. An important part of obedience training is helping the owner to enjoy and work well with their dog. Dog trainers also train dogs and their owners to compete in obedience trials.

Teaching dog obedience classes is not high-paying work. Because most owners work during the day, classes need to be held on evenings or weekends. Finding an appropriate rental facility may be difficult; some landlords are not happy to have dogs as tenants. Insurance, utilities, and advertising add additional expenses.

Show Dogs. Dogs who are trained for shows must be taught to walk, stand, and move in ways that comply with show rules. They must learn to demonstrate the characteristics and conformation for which they will be judged. Dogs must be able to maintain a pose if judges seek a closer examination or wish to examine their teeth.

Trainers of show dogs need to attend shows, talk with show trainers, and learn as much as possible about the essentials of showing dogs; learning also comes through courses or seminars. One way show trainers build a reputation is by competing successfully with their own dogs, which they have trained.

Therapy Dogs. Dogs have long been known for their willingness to help humans, but only recently have they been used in therapy.

Studies have shown that humans with pets—whether dogs, cats, or other pets such as rabbits—have lower blood pressure, are better able to release strain and tension, and are less lonely. The pet visitation program, in which pets and pet owners go to rehabilitation centers, retirement centers, and other facilities, has been especially helpful for lonely or withdrawn persons.

More recently, therapists have used dogs that have passed certification examinations to help in treating patients who have serious conditions. One example is aphasia—a loss of ability to understand or speak due to brain damage, which is usually caused by an accident. In therapy, persons with aphasia who like dogs may relax more in their presence, and the act of responding to a dog helps take their mind off their own difficulties in speaking. Most often these dogs are owned by the therapists and they supplement the work of the therapist for a day or so a week.

Therapy dogs or other pets can help special needs children overcome emotional problems and physical challenges. Caring for and working with animals also help some children gain self-esteem. This has been shown to be particularly helpful for autistic or abused children. Additionally, animals have been used as a part of rehabilitation in some prison settings.

Trainers of therapy dogs need to first train their dogs in obedience. Dogs also need to be desensitized to certain aspects of hospital or rehabilitation center environments—such as machine noises—so that they can concentrate on the task at hand. One organization that administers certification examinations to dogs is Therapy Dogs International; the test is known as the Canine Good Citizen Test. Along with the Delta Society, it also provides information about training programs.

Service Dogs. Training service dogs is intensive work, involving many long and tedious days of training; it may even involve living in dorms with the dogs. Service, or assistance, dogs are quite different from therapy dogs. These dogs help people with physical and medical disabilities in their day-to-day existence: guiding the blind, acting as an ear for the deaf, pulling a wheelchair, alerting individuals to the presence of an intruder, and providing rescue or protection work (such as activating an alert system or barking for help). They may also fetch dropped items, warn the individual of an impending seizure, operate light switches, open doors, and assist with roll-over in bed. Some can even cushion against a fall. The tasks these dogs do are essential to the well-being of their owners and allow them to live independently. When a service dog is trained and ready to be placed, the dog trainers shift the focus of their work. The next stage is to teach the people who will use these dogs how to interact with them.

No specific educational requirements exist for these dog trainers, but good qualifying backgrounds are degrees in psychology or human services and previous experience working with animals and people who have disabilities. Valuable experience for this work can also come from volunteering to raise puppies that will go into the program. (Not only is it important for these dogs to have a nurturing home, but in the process they can be given new experiences that help prepare them for their work as service dogs.) Service dog trainers spend some time, usually three years, apprenticing with an experienced trainer or working as an assistant. Some governments require that these dog trainers pass exams; prospective trainers will need to know the requirements for their state or province.

While a few private organizations offer jobs for service dog trainers, most employment opportunities are offered by Guide Dogs for the Blind (GDB). These opportunities are usually for instructor assistants, apprentice instructors, and licensed instructors. People who are interested in a career as a licensed instructor should apply for the entry-level position of instructor assistant. After they have met certain requirements they may be accepted into GBD's three-year apprenticeship program.

Virtually all service dog schools are non-profit, so the pay for training these dogs is not high. At GDB, apprentice instructors begin at about $30,000, licensed instructors begin at about $36,000, and senior instructors can make as much as $79,000. Most individuals enter this type of work because of the rewards of working with dogs and in helping other people. Because the field is quite small and openings come up very rarely, jobs training service dogs are very competitive.

Search and Rescue Dogs. Search and rescue (SAR) dogs are trained to find the scent of a human in the air—or sometimes on the ground—in order to locate people who are lost in the wilderness or are victims of disasters such as avalanches, earthquakes, floods, explosions, or tornadoes. They may also help to find forensic evidence at crime scenes or parts of an airplane after a crash. SAR dogs are able to work in places where other searchers have been; in heavily populated areas containing many different smells, they can search if given an object with the scent of the missing person. Neither the weather nor the time of day limits these dogs. They are especially effective in situations where human sight is limited: in the dark, in heavy brush or dense woods, in debris (such as is found after tornadoes and floods or in collapsed buildings), and under water.

Virtually all SAR units—dogs and trainers alike—volunteer their time. In some cases the human part of the unit is a police officer called to provide SAR in times of need. SAR units often travel across the United States or to other countries that have experienced a disaster of some kind. The most common scenario is that the trainer owns the dog and learns to train it by following books and other printed information and working with volunteer trainers who have more experience.

Trainers of these dogs, or dog handlers, must enjoy being outdoors in any kind of weather, and they must especially enjoy working with dogs. They need a high level of physical fitness and must be able to respond quickly to emergencies; this means the ability to immediately leave their work and go to the site. They must understand land navigation and be able to use map, compass, and radio communications. They must also have wilderness survival skills, a knowledge of basic first aid, and, often, advanced first aid techniques such as cardiopulmonary resuscitation. Before a dog and a handler are sent on any search missions, other teams evaluate them to ensure that they are ready.

SAR dogs need to be trainable, have agility and endurance, not be overly aggressive, and be able to get along with other dogs and with people. The most common breeds used are the larger working and sporting dogs: German shepherds, rottweilers, giant schnauzers, dobermans, golden retrievers, and labradors. Search dogs are members of the handler's family and consider people to be friends. Usually the training of these dogs begins when they are puppies, although an older dog that has a good working relationship with the handler may also be used. Minimum time for training is usually a year with training sessions at least twice a week.

The National Search and Rescue Organization estimates that more than 150 air-scenting search dog units have been formed throughout the United States, and more are being formed. Although different units may use somewhat different methods, the basic concept of using air-scenting dogs is uniform. This allows the agencies that request the dogs to know how best to use them in the field and for different teams to work together well in a large-scale search.

Security Dogs and Police Dogs. Dogs are used by many police departments as part of K-9 units, where they are used to track and help to capture suspected criminals, to locate drugs or bombs by sniffing, and to search for missing persons or victims of crimes or disasters.

Police dog handlers usually train their own dogs, which entails going to training camps and seminars. They need to work in all kinds of weather and circumstances. When they are not on duty, the dogs live in their homes as family pets. To work effectively on the job, the quality of the training that both the police officer and the dogs receive is important. Many organizations provide training courses for these security or police dogs and their handlers. Police dog handlers must qualify for police work before going on to handle dogs.

In many cases, volunteer search and rescue teams provide dogs to police departments instead of the departments keeping the dogs themselves. People who work on these teams can be involved in search and rescue without the necessity of becoming a police officer. Other organizations provide all of the services—both dogs and handlers—for security or bomb and drug detection.

The use of security dogs is not confined to police departments. All branches of the military also use dogs for different security purposes. Information on this can be gained by contacting any recruiting office. In airports, dogs sniff for bombs and explosives, and they provide security at various businesses.

Cats. People commonly believe that cats cannot be trained. Indeed, training cats is not as straightforward as training dogs and many other animals: they tend to be more independent than dogs and less inclined to please a trainer. But it is possible to train cats. The cats in movies and on television, for example, have been very carefully trained to follow certain cues to produce specific actions.

Cat training, like the training of many other animals, involves the use of food as a reward and a clicker—a small, plastic toy that associates the reward with a sound and reinforces the desired behavior. However, even a well-trained cat may refuse to cooperate. For a movie or TV shoot, a trainer will always have several trained cats on hand and use the one that is in a cooperative mood.

Cat trainers work for TV and movie producers. Some have their own touring animal shows that may include many kinds of animals. The cat food manufacturer Friskies often has a cat trainer appear at various cat shows and other such events to demonstrate training methods and show off the trained cats.

Although training animals for movies or television programs may seem glamorous and exciting, it is actually very hard work. Before arriving on the set for a shoot the animals require long hours of preparation and weeks of training. On the set there are long waits, the possibility of numerous retakes and other complications, and a day that begins before dawn with loading and transporting animals and necessary equipment, including food and water. The day ends with the drive back, unloading the animals at their facility, feeding and watering them, and cleaning the transport equipment before you can go home. A shoot may last fourteen hours or more—this is definitely not a nine-to-five job.

Although those jobs may seem lucrative, the pay can be quite low unless the trainer is a union member. Because the work is highly competitive and the job-seekers outnumber the openings, some trainers may volunteer their work free just to get a foot in the door. In fact, the animal's owner may make more money than a trainer, although trainers receive the money if they own the animal.

Cats are trained for other functions as well. They can be trained to walk on a leash, to jump through hoops, to curl up in a ball upon command, and various other tricks usually associated only with dogs. Young kittens can be trained to use the litter box, though this comes very naturally to most cats and is usually done by the mother. Some cats have even been trained to use a toilet instead of a litter box.

See profile on page 45.
Additional trainer information on pages 64, 84, 88, and 101.

ANIMAL CONTROL OFFICER

Salary Range: Nationwide average is $24,450 to $29,000.
Educational Requirements: Some states require informal training, others train after hiring; persons with no experience may be hired. Law and security are helpful courses.
Employment Outlook: Average.

In general, animal control officers work to provide a safe environment for the human and animal populations. They promote the safe treatment of animals, and may be called if an animal has been left in a closed car in hot weather or if people are taunting or abusing creatures in public parks. They may write tickets for unlicensed dogs and impound stray dogs found roaming the streets.

Animal control officers work with local communities to protect both wild and domestic animals. They do everything from removing abused pets from homes to tracking down and capturing diseased wildlife that pose a danger to humans and other animals. They meet with pet owners, speak with neighbors, and investigate claims of abuse. If they find an abused pet, they can issue fines and even take the owner to court.

As part of their work, these officers also help to educate the public about animal care, animal welfare, and the protection services available in the community. They promote spaying and neutering, raise awareness of the dangers of abandoning animals, and may try to find caring homes for former strays (or care for the animals themselves, especially if they work from a pound or kennel).

Animal control officers typically deal with complaints from community members and follow up on these issues. If a law has been violated, they need to take actions to solve the situation, including explaining the law to violators. They may need to take actions if law enforcement orders are not followed, such as issuing tickets, summons, and subpoenas. To this end they need to carefully document all actions in case of a trial or a repeat violation.

Animal control officers need to be able to work with frightened, injured, or hostile creatures, and thus they must be healthy and strong and love all animals. They should be good communicators and keen observers of detail. They also must understand laws regarding animals and be able to solve problems, resolve conflicts, and negotiate.

Officers risk bites and infection, as they may be exposed to diseased and frightened animals. They work both indoors and outdoors, in all kinds of weather, and may have to do shift work that includes nights, weekends, and holidays. Animal control officers may work alone or, depending on the size of the community, in teams.

Most employers for animal control officers are state or local governments. The state regulations that they must enforce come mostly from the department of agriculture. While some work for city police departments or county sheriff's departments, others work for a private company or organization contracted to fulfill this function. Some universities hire these workers, as at the University of California at Santa Cruz. Volunteer experience with a local Humane Society chapter or the

Society for Prevention of Cruelty to Animals is good background and gives one an advantage in obtaining jobs.

In some locations the work is part-time. Because the exact structure and responsibilities of the work vary from location to location, individuals interested in this type of work should research local possibilities. Work as an animal control officer may lead to supervisor positions or police work. Officers may also go to law or veterinary school or become animal rights activists.

The National Animal Control Association has been working since its founding in 1978 to advance the professionalism of this career. The organization offers courses and provides an annual training conference to help animal control personnel learn to correct problems in their communities that result from irresponsible animal ownership, and to encourage responsible ownership.

BOARDING KENNEL OPERATOR

Salary Range: Generally low and usually balanced with
    other work such as grooming.
Educational Requirements: Experience with animals is most
    essential.
Employment Outlook: Expected to remain steady.

Kennels board animals—mostly dogs, although some cats and other small creatures are boarded—while the owners are at work or away from home. Attendants provide the day-to-day care of these animals. The work involves cleaning the cages and dog runs, feeding and watering the animals, and exercising them. Experienced attendants may provide a more advanced level of care, including basic medical attention and grooming details such as bathing and nail trimming.

Boarding kennel operators must deal with many different business details. They need to work well with people so that their clients return and provide good word-of-mouth advertising. They need to ensure that the kennel is clean and disease-free. Most of all, they need to have a great concern for the well-being of the dogs and other animals in their care.

Especially busy times for kennel operators are the summer months and school holidays. Some kennels sell pet food and supplies or provide other services such as helping with breeding or preparing animals for shipping. Kennel work involves weekend hours as animals need to be fed and cared for every day.

PET GROOMER

Salary Range: Median pay is $25,907. Self-employed pet groomers often work long hours but can earn anywhere from $15,000 to $50,000 a year.

Educational Requirements: No certification is required; some schools of grooming exist, and seminars on grooming are available. Previous animal care experience essential, but training is mainly on the job.

Employment Outlook: Excellent.

Pet groomers are individuals who specialize in maintaining the appearance of pets, usually dogs or cats. Their work involves a number of steps, beginning with an initial brush-out and first clipping of hair or fur. This is followed by nail cutting, ear cleaning, and bathing and drying (often blow-drying). The last step is a final round of clipping and styling. Tools used for this work include electric clippers, combs, and grooming shears. Professional groomers can administer baths and flea dips, when needed, and clip cat claws—a task that can be quite difficult for owners.

Pet groomers work with both owners and pets. It is important that groomers first spend time with the owners to learn the type of styling the owner expects and any special pet grooming needs. They next need to spend time with the pet, evaluating its disposition and interpreting its personality. Then they use this information as a guide for the grooming they do. Groomers are also front-line animal care workers who may notice medical problems that require veterinary care—such as an ear or skin infection—before owners do.

Pet groomers need to understand animal behavior, so previous animal care experience is very important, as is on-the-job training or a certificate in grooming. One way to get into the field is to work part-time during the busiest seasons—spring and summer.

Pet groomers need to be healthy and physically fit. They need to have a real love of animals, so that they do not find cleaning up after them a chore. Pet groomers must be able to maintain control of the animals while at the same time being gentle and patient. Creativity and an artistic sensibility are very important, especially with animals that require a specialized look. It is also essential that pet groomers are not allergic to dogs or cats.

The work of groomers is most in evidence at dog or cat shows, but groomers are also important for reasons other than fashion or show prizes. Although cats are very fastidious and most do not need professional grooming, some do. A groomer may be needed, for example, for long-haired outdoor (and even some indoor) cats, whose fur is easily matted. Some cats are superficial groomers, and cats that are old or have physical problems may not be able to groom themselves adequately. In these cases, owners may find it very difficult to groom their own cats.

Groomers may elect to specialize in either dogs or cats, and they may gain a reputation as being good with one or the other. Although more dogs than cats are taken to groomers, the number of cats taken to groomers is increasing. This trend may present a good opportunity for the person who prefers to work with cats. Because cats are more difficult to groom than dogs—they have "more armor," says one cat groomer—a good groomer must be able to read cat body language. People who love and know cats will be better able to read that language and to work with a cat.

At this time, licensing is not required to enter this field, but courses and seminars on grooming are available. These can be especially helpful in learning the business details of a self-owned pet grooming business. Additionally, membership in a professional organization, and certification through that organization, will lend authority and professionalism to the practitioner. Such certification may in fact become a necessity as the field expands.

Pet groomers work in different settings. Kennels often hire dog groomers. Some veterinary clinics have grooming services, as do some pet-supply stores, and some animal shelters use pet groomers. Many individuals operate their own pet-grooming business. Some groomers will come to homes to groom a cat in order to make the animal comfortable; a cat may be more inclined to be cooperative if the stresses of traveling to, and being in, a strange setting are removed.

This is a growing field, with an employment increase of twelve percent expected through to 2010. The U.S. Department of Labor predicts that pet owners, including baby boomers who are expected to have a good retirement income, will take increasing advantage of pet-grooming services.

PET SITTER
Salary Range: Varies tremendously; well-established busi-
    nesses can be quite profitable.
Educational Requirements: Proper training, through avail-
    able courses, is important. A course in pet first aid is rec-
    ommended.
Employment Outlook: This is a growth field. Most sitters
    own their own businesses, but some work for others.

A love of animals and the ability to work with animals—perhaps
a variety of species, depending on how the business is set up—are the
essential ingredients for individuals who enter this career. Pet sitting
is an excellent way to transfer a love of animals into paid work. It can
also be a good career choice for individuals who love animals but for
various reasons are not able to have them in their homes or apart-
ments. Some pet sitters specialize in only one type of animal—cats, for
example. However, many simply bill themselves as pet-sitters and provide services for dogs, cats, and other small animals.

Many pets are most comfortable in their own home where they
can follow their usual routines. This is especially true of cats. Owners
often use pet sitters to care for their pets in their home environment
when they take vacations. Use of a pet sitter ensures that animals are
not stressed by being in a cage in a strange place with strange animals
nearby, and that they are not exposed to germs from these animals. An
additional benefit for owners who use sitters is the security that comes
from having someone visit the home while they are away. Sitters can
check that doors and windows are secure and hide an owner's absence
by alternating lights and blinds and bringing in mail and newspapers.

Establishing a pet sitting business involves some legal expenses.
Pet owners need to be bonded by an insurance company—which pro-
tects the homeowners against theft—in addition to insuring themselves. This covers the pet sitter in case something happens to the pet
in the sitter's care.

Pet sitting can pay well. But it takes time to attract enough cus-
tomers to support a business. Individuals who are beginning their own
business should have another means of support until they have a well-
established client base.

SHELTER WORKER

Salary Range: Varies tremendously. The pay is higher for larger shelters and shelters where staff is unionized. There is no standard of pay for managers. Other staff are usually paid by the hour. A common pay range for a medium-size shelter is $12 to $17 an hour, depending on position and duties.

Educational Requirements: No educational requirements; secondary or post-secondary training or certification gives an advantage to job-seekers.

Employment Outlook: Demand is expected to remain steady.

The jobs at animal shelters, where stray and unclaimed animals are taken, range from the managers down to the workers, or caretakers, and include work for volunteers.

Shelter managers are essentially supervisors who oversee the shelter's operations and ensure that daily care is provided to the animals. They may take direct care of animals received into the shelter, making sure that they receive health care and vaccinations. They also work with the people who come in to adopt an animal or deliver one to the shelter. They need to have supervisory skills, as they must supervise the direct-care workers and volunteers, and they need to be able to work well with both people and animals. Shelter managers also need to be able to coordinate with other organizations, as many animal shelters work closely with social service agencies and law enforcement teams.

Caretakers have a variety of tasks and work with many different animals. They must take care of the animals' basic needs and keep records of animals received, animals discharged, and any tests or treatments administered. They may vaccinate newly admitted animals, as directed by a veterinarian or veterinary technician, and they may euthanize animals that are severely ill or injured or have been unclaimed after a certain length of time. Caretakers also interact with the public. They answer the telephone, screen prospective applicants for animal adoption, and educate visitors on animal health issues such as neutering and spaying.

While no specialized training is required, training programs are increasingly becoming available through organizations such as the Humane Society of the United States, the American Humane Association, and the National Animal Control Association. Workshop topics include investigating cruelty to animals and preventing wildlife problems. With a combination of experience and this type of training, caretakers may advance to positions in larger organizations such as adoption coordinator, animal control officer, emergency rescue driver, assistant shelter manager, or shelter manager.

Most workers in shelters are volunteers. Volunteering to groom, exercise, socialize, and clean at animal shelters is a good way to learn if you can work with dogs or other small animals every day. And animal lovers may simply find it to be pleasurable work.

DOG SHOWS

Dog shows most likely began in a small way, as an attempt to determine bragging rights for owning the best local dog. They are now a big business. The American Kennel Club (AKC) lists many different types of dog shows. These include obedience trials, field trials, agility trials, herding trials, hunting tests, and tracking tests. Shows may judge the dogs on their instincts, as in herding trials, as well as on trainability, as in obedience shows. Most common, however, are conformation dog shows, which evaluate the overall appearance, build, and, in some breeds, temperament of a dog against the standards set for that particular breed. The best-known dog show in North America is the Westminster Dog Show, a conformation dog show, which is one of the continent's longest continuously held sporting events, second only to the Kentucky Derby. The show has been held every year since the founding of the Westminster Kennel Club in 1877.

The AKC recognizes some 150 breeds of dogs and certifies registration papers that list the parentage of each dog as proof of its purebred status. Dog shows may specialize in one breed or in all breeds.

PROFESSIONAL DOG HANDLER

Salary Range: Varies considerably.

Educational Requirements: Long experience with showing dogs and an apprenticeship with a well-known handler.

Employment Outlook: As dog shows increase in number, so will the work for handlers.

Many owners show their own purebred dogs. However, some owners cannot travel to the many shows necessary to obtain the awards or championship points they want for their dogs, or simply do not wish to show their dogs themselves. This is where professional dog handlers find their work: clients pay these professionals to show their dogs. Handlers usually travel with several dogs and enter them in shows almost every weekend.

Dog handlers need to be able to work well with dogs, and they must understand the different breeds and the point system by which they will be judged. Because this is hard work, handlers must be in good shape, and they must work every day to maintain the dogs' physical and mental health. In particular, they have to make sure that the dogs know how to stand and show their movement, that they have an attractive coat, and that they will otherwise meet the breed standards. Because each dog is in the ring only about two minutes, handlers must prepare well. (The ring is the area where the different classes, such as Puppy or American-Bred, are shown.)

Handlers also need people and money skills, as their best means of advertising is word of mouth from satisfied clients. They must negotiate contracts with clients, which can be quite complicated, usually involving travel expenses and boarding fees. Handlers may use some of their payment for paying assistants to handle the dogs daily and for food and other expenses. The handler's salary comes after all expenses have been paid, so it is essential that he or she understands the costs involved and includes them in the contract.

People interested in handling should consider first working as an assistant to ensure that they do enjoy the demanding work and travel schedule. Professional dog handlers usually spend a long time as apprentices, often up to ten years. Membership in a professional handlers' association comes with strict requirements—successful membership applicants must have significant experience as handlers and meet other rigid standards. These professional associations are on the cutting edge of developing professionalism among dog handlers and cultivating the respect that is due someone with this expertise.

DOG SHOW JUDGE

Salary Range: AKC delegates, representing member clubs, may judge but receive only show expenses—travel, parking, tolls, motels, meals, and so on. Most starting judges receive $3 per dog; fees paid to judges can progress from $100 to $600 a day, plus expenses.

Educational Requirements: Must pass the test of the licensing organization and take courses and seminars; AKC judges must have a documented twelve years of experience with dogs.

Employment Outlook: Work for good judges will always be available; judges qualified for judging more breeds will have more work.

Dog show judges have to be registered with the organization sponsoring an event and meet the qualifications for judges set by that organization. In North America, the two major organizations are the American Kennel Club and the Canadian Kennel Club, but other organizations also sponsor dog shows.

The purpose of conformation shows is to evaluate the breeding stock and ensure the purity and continued high standards for each breed. In fact, judges do not compare dogs to their competitors in the ring, but rather to the ideal for that particular breed. They observe the dog's gait, or movement, examine the teeth to see that they align well, and look at bone structure and proportions. If the breed standard specifies coat texture, muscle conditioning, and temperament, judges also look for these qualities. Many judges specialize in several breeds while others are qualified to judge all breeds.

The best background for dog show judges is breeding and exhibiting dogs—hands-on experience is essential. By carefully observing at dog shows, talking with judges and breeders, and using some of the excellent written resources that are available, individuals can gain important background information. Each parent club has standards, and many have seminars or courses for judges.

One of the hurdles to becoming a judge is a written test. Judges who pass the written test are known as "permit" or "provisional" judges; they are carefully evaluated on the job and must successfully complete a certain number of judging assignments before being allowed to judge without evaluation. Evaluators check whether the judge follows the proper ring procedure and policies and determine whether the judge has an adequate knowledge of the standards for the breed being judged.

In addition to the extensive background needed to pass certification, judges need to be able to concentrate in a setting with background noise and lots of activity. Judges must be confident of their abilities and they should project an air of confidence and authority.

Some judges work full-time. For most, however, judging dog shows is part-time work. Many judges travel great distances to events and work for little more than the compensation they receive for expenses. A few judges, whose main concern is maintaining the purity of a specific breed or breeds, simply volunteer their time.

See profile on page 48.

Other Dog Show Work

In addition to dog handlers and judges, other work at a dog show helps ensure a well-run show. Some of these are paying jobs while others provide only a small stipend or are volunteer work. Persons interested in any of these types of work should attend dog shows and talk with the people working at the show. As always, the experts are the people doing the actual work. However, the work can vary a great deal from location to location and can depend on the size of the show.

Show Superintendent. Show superintendents handle details that are necessary for a dog show to run smoothly. Superintendents are in charge of getting the entry form (the "premium list") printed and mailed to prospective exhibitors. They draw up the show program, allotting times for judging each show, and mail the program to each registrant. If a show does not have a secretary, which is usually a volunteer job, the show superintendent also handles those responsibilities.

Superintendents are also in charge of furnishing the physical equipment needed for the show. This includes the mats, ring standards, and barriers and special equipment such as ramps for the smaller breeds. If breed standards include height and weight requirements, superintendents obtain wickets to measure for height requirements and scales for weighing. They also ensure that the necessary ribbons and armbands are ready for the show.

Superintendents are essential to run a show effectively. They are usually members of an organization that is licensed by the AKC to provide these services.

Dog Show Photographer. The show committee hires dog show photographers, but the individuals whose dogs are photographed on request pay the photographers for their pictures. Generally, these photographers take pictures of the winners, but they may also photograph other dogs, if desired by dog owners. The amount a photographer earns per show depends on the size of the show. Small shows may only yield ten to forty shots, but an all-breed show could generate sixty to one hundred fifty. Some photographers specialize and photograph only dog shows and they find the work quite remunerative. This is a highly competitive field, but several factors can give new photographers an opportunity to start in the field: an increase in the number and types of dog shows, the retirement of older photographers, and decisions to replace photographers because of substandard work.

Steward. The stewards in a dog show assist the judges, freeing them to concentrate on evaluating the dogs. Stewards help keep the show running on time, minimize delays between events, maintain show records, clean the ring, and give judges ribbons and trophies to hand out. When necessary, they contact other show officials, such as the photographer, veterinarians, superintendent, or clean-up crews. Stewards also handle details relating to exhibitors, such as handing out armbands, answering questions, and calling exhibitors into the ring at the beginning of a show. Exhibitors must view each steward as an impartial, helpful assistant. Stewards must remember that they are only helpers to judges, not advisors, and they must be careful not to appear to influence a judge's decision.

The steward is a volunteer position, although some stewards may receive a small payment or simply a free lunch. If necessary, professional steward clubs can supply stewards for large shows or for small clubs with no available volunteers.

Show Secretary. Show secretaries receive the entries for the show and prepare the catalog for printing. Show secretaries usually are members of the local dog club sponsoring the show. Not all shows have secretaries, and in these situations the show superintendents handle these functions. Like steward, show secretary is a volunteer position.

CAT SHOWS

There are a number of jobs involved with showing cats. These are not full-time jobs, but are performed by persons who have other employment. Indeed, some of them are volunteer positions and may be performed by students seeking show experience. Clerks and stewards are usually always volunteer roles. Each organization that sponsors a show has its own requirements for judges and its own standards of remuneration.

Judge. As one of the officials who evaluates the entrants at a cat show, a show judge must be very experienced. Each organization that sponsors cat shows has its own specific training program to ensure that the judges in their shows are well qualified for their role. The Cat Fanciers' Association (CFA), for example, requires judges to have ten years of experience in breeding cats, a knowledge of how cats should be exhibited, and prior work in shows as a show manager, entry clerk, ring clerk, or master clerk. In short, they must be thoroughly knowledgeable about every aspect of cat shows. Demonstrated moral character is also important.

After a potential judge meets the background qualifications, he or she can apply to a judging program. Once accepted into the program, trainees must pass examinations on breed standards and the mechanics of show rings. They also need to apprentice with experienced instructors.

Clerks, Master and Ring. The master clerk has the responsibility of consolidating the awards on judges' sheets for all of the rings into a master catalog. (The master catalog is the official record of the show; it contains the count of the various categories of cats and kittens that were present and competing in that show.) He or she also ensures that the judges' sheets are complete and accurate and resolves any potential errors before the judge has left the ring. Another responsibility of the master clerk is to make any corrections in the master catalog that have been requested by exhibitors.

Ring clerks work with both the judge and the exhibitors. Under the direction of the judge, they manage the operation of a specific ring; this includes supervising the stewards and calling for and sending back the cats for judging in a particular class. Ring clerks ensure that judges' decisions are correctly recorded. After the judge, the ring clerk is the second most important person in a judging ring. Ring clerks anticipate the needs of the judge, working to minimize distractions and maintain good relations with the exhibitors. Clerks often use the manuals and forms that CFA has developed to help them perform their functions at a show.

Steward. Each ring has one steward assigned to it. Before a cat is placed in a judging cage, a steward must thoroughly clean the cage with a disinfectant and deodorizing solution. This cleaning helps to prevent diseases from being transferred from one cat to another. Cages are also cleaned at the beginning of the day. Each cage must be thoroughly dry before a cat is placed in it.

Stewarding duties at a show may be done by members of service organizations—girl or boy scout troops, 4-H clubs, and so forth—as a way to earn money for their group. For some of these organizations, participants also earn badges from this kind of work. High school students looking for volunteer experience sometimes work as stewards, too.

RESOURCES
General

American Kennel Club
P.O. Box 3790
Raleigh, NC 27606
job line: 919-816-3896
fax: 919-816-4287
www.akc.org

Canadian Cat Association/L'Association Féline
Canadienne
289 Rutherford Road, S, #18
Brampton, Ontario
Canada L6W 3R9
phone: 905-459-1481
fax: 905-459-4023
email: office@cca-afc.com
www.cca-afc.com

Canadian Kennel Club/Club Canin Canadien
Commerce Court
89 Skyway Avenue, Suite 100
Etobicoke, Ontario
Canada M9W 6R4
phone: 416-675-5511
fax: 416-675-6506
email: information@ckc.ca
www.ckc.ca

Cat Fancier's Association
P.O. Box 1005
Manasquan, NJ 08736-0805
phone: 732-528-9797
fax: 732-528-7391
email: cfa@cfa.org
www.cfainc.org

Companion Animal Protection Society (CAPS)
PMB 143
2100 West Drake Road
Fort Collins, CO 80526
phone: 970-223-8300
fax: 970-223-8330
email: caps@caps-web.org
www.caps-web.org

International Cat Association
P.O. Box 2684
Harlingen, TX 78551
phone: 956-428-8046
fax: 956-428-8047
email: ticaeo@xanadu2.net
www.tica.org

Grooming

National Dog Groomers Association of America
P.O. Box 101
Clark, PA 16113
phone: 724-962-2711
fax: 724-962-1919
email: ndga@nationaldoggroomers.com
www.nationaldoggroomers.com

Professional Handling

Professional Handler's Association
17017 Norbrook Drive
Onley, MD 20832
phone: 301-924-0089
www.infodog.com/misc/pha/phainfo.htm

Pet Sitting

Canadian Pet Sitters Association
email: information@petsitcanada.com
www.petsitcanada.com

National Association of Professional Pet Sitters
17000 Commerce Parkway, Suite C
Mt. Laurel, NJ 08054
phone: 856-439-0324
fax: 856-439-0525
email: napps@ahint.com
www.petsitters.org

Pet Sitters International
201 East King Street
King, NC 27021-9161
phone: 336-983-9222
fax: 336-983-5266
email: info@petsit.com
www.petsit.com

Animal Control/Shelters

American Society for the Prevention of Cruelty
to Animals (ASPCA)
424 East 92nd Street
New York, NY 10128
fax: 212-876-0014
www.aspca.org

National Animal Control Association
P.O. Box 480851
Kansas City, MO 64148
phone: 913-768-1319
fax: 913-768-1378
email: naca@interserv.com
www.nacanet.org

Boarding Kennels

American Boarding Kennels Association
1702 East Pikes Peak Avenue
Colorado Springs, CO 80909
phone: 719-667-1600
fax: 719-667-0116
email: info@abka.com
www.abka.com

General Training

American Dog Trainers Network
phone: 212-727-7257
email: dogs@inch.com
www.inch.com/~dogs/

Association of Pet Dog Trainers
5096 Sand Road SE
Iowa City, IA 52240-8217
phone: 800-738-3647
fax: 856-439-0525
email: information@apdt.com
www.apdt.com

Directory of Virginia Dog Clubs, All Breed Kennels,
Breed Specialty Clubs, Obedience Clubs, and
Specialized Training Clubs
www.barkbytes.com

International Association of Canine Professionals
P.O. Box 560156
Montverde, FL 34756-0156
phone: 407-469-2008
email: iacp@mindspring.com
www.dogpro.org
K-911: Dog Training Resource Page
www.geocities.com/jetflair/index.html

Obedience Training

National Association of Dog Obedience Instructors
PMB 369
729 Grapevine Highway
Hurst, TX 76054-2085
www.nadoi.org

Service/Assistance Dogs

> Blue Ridge Assistance Dogs
> 8600 Smith Lane
> Manassas, VA 20112
> phone: 703-369-5878
> www.blueridgeassistancedogs.org
>
> Canine Companions for Independence
> P.O. Box 446
> Santa Rosa, CA 95402-0446
> phone: 800-572-2275
> email: info@caninecompanions.org
> www.caninecompanions.org
>
> Delta Society
> 875 124th Avenue, NW, Suite 101
> Bellevue, WA 98005-2531
> phone: 425-226-7357
> fax: 425-235-1076
> email: info@deltasociety.org
> www.deltasociety.org
>
> Dogs for the Deaf
> 10175 Wheeler Road
> Central Point, OR 97502
> phone: 541-826-9220
> fax: 541-826-6696
> email: info@dogsforthedeaf.org
> www.dogsforthedeaf.org
>
> Guide Dogs for the Blind
> P.O. Box 151200
> San Rafael, CA 94915-1200
> job line: 800-295-4050 (x 4011)
> www.guidedogs.com

Loving Paws Assistance Dogs
P.O. Box 12005
Santa Rosa, CA 95406
phone: 707-586-0798
fax: 707-586-0799
email: info@lovingpaws.org
www.lovingpaws.org

Pacific Assistance Dogs Society
9048 Stormont Avenue
Burnaby, British Columbia
Canada V3N 4G6
phone: 604-527-0556
fax: 604-527-0558
email: info@padsdogs.org
www.padsdogs.org

Paws With a Cause
4646 South Division
Wayland, MI 49348
phone: 800-253-7297
fax: 616-877-0248
email: paws@ionline.com
www.ismi.net/paws

Puppyworks
P.O. Box 954
Benicia, CA 94510
phone: 707-745-4237
fax: 707-745-8310
email: events@puppyworks.com
www.puppyworks.com

Therapy Dogs International (TDI)
88 Bartley Road
Flanders, NJ 07836
phone: 973-252-9800
fax: 973-252-7171
email: tdi@gti.net
www.tdi-dog.org

Training for Stage and Screen

> International Alliance of Theatrical Stage Employees,
> Moving Picture Technicians, Artists and Allied Crafts
> of the United States, Its Territories and Canada
> 1430 Broadway, 20th Floor
> New York, NY 10018
> phone: 212-730-1770
> fax: 212-730-7809
> www.iatse-intl.org

Police/Customs/Security Dog Training

> International Association of Bomb Technicians and
> Investigators
> P.O. Box 160
> Goldvein, VA 22720-0160
> phone: 540-752-4533
> fax: 540-752-2796
> email: admin@iabti.org
> www.iabti.org

> National Narcotic Detector Dog Association
> 379 CR 105
> Carthage, TX 75633
> email: nnddasecretary@yahoo.com
> www.nndda.org

> North American Police Work Dog Association
> (NAPWDA)
> 4222 Manchester Avenue
> Perry, OH 44081
> phone: 888-422-6463
> fax: 440-259-3170 (*51)
> www.napwda.com

> United States Police Canine Association (USPCA)
> P.O. Box 80
> Springboro, OH 45066
> phone: 800-531-1614
> www.uspcak9.com

U.S. Customs Service Canine Enforcement Training
Center
phone: 888-872-3641
email: canine@customs.treas.gov
www.customs.ustreas.gov/enforcem/k9.htm

Search-and-Rescue Training

National Association for Search and Rescue
4500 Southgate Place, Suite 100
Chantilly, VA 20151-1714
phone: 888-893-7788
fax: 703-222-6283
email: info@nasar.org
www.nasar.org

Law Enforcement Bloodhound Association
P.O. Box 471267
Aurora, CO 80047-1267
phone: 303-369-6784
email: manhunters@comcast.net
www.leba98.com

Training Newsletters and Magazines

Front and Finish
phone: 309-344-1333
www.frontandfinish.com

Off-Lead
Barkleigh Productions
6 State Road, #113
Mechanicsburg, PA 17055
phone: 717-691-3388
fax: 717-691-3381
email: info@barkleigh.com
www.off-lead.com

The Clicker Journal
20146 Gleedsville Road
Leesburg, VA 20175
www.clickertrain.com

Clean Run
Clean Run Productions
35 North Chicopee Street
Chicopee, MA 01020
phone: 800-311-6503
fax: 413-532-1590
email: info@cleanrun.com
www.cleanrun.com

Show Judging

American Dog Show Judges
www.adsj.org

Canadian Dog Judges Association
983 Ormsby Street
London, Ontario
Canada N6Z 1K6
www.dogjudge.com

Other Small Pets

American Rabbit Breeders Association
P.O. Box 426
Bloomington, IL 61702
phone: 309-664-7500
fax: 309-664-0941
email: arbapost@aol.com
www.arba.net

Alberta Ferret Society
P.O. Box 68209
162 Bonnie Doon Mall
Edmonton, Alberta, Canada T6C 4N6
phone: 877-337-7380
www.albertaferretsociety.com

American Ferret Association
PMB 255
626-C Admiral Drive
Annapolis, MD 21401
phone: 888-337-7381
fax: 516-908-5215
email: afa@ferret.org
www.ferret.org

Profile

HIMALAYAN CAT AND ALPACA BREEDER
Bonnie McNamara

"I always knew I would work with animals, since my love for them was so strong," says Bonnie McNamara. She was involved with animals throughout her childhood and youth—dogs, cats, bunnies, and, later, horses. McNamara's current occupation—breeding Himalayan cats and alpacas on twenty acres of land just outside Ottawa, Ontario—is a logical progression from her experiences growing up. She defines her work as "breeding and raising healthy Himalayans to both provide loving pets for people and to better the breed itself." When she branched out in 1998 and added alpacas, one of the factors that influenced her choice was the fact that alpacas are raised for their wool and as breeding stock. "I could not raise livestock that would eventually end up slaughtered," she says.

"Breeding and raising animals is a full-time job," McNamara says. "Your day begins with chores and ends with chores." She spends hours every day vacuuming and cleaning, "to keep the premises as sterile as possible to prevent disease," and cleans litter boxes three times daily. Then she feeds, waters, grooms, medicates the animals that need medication, and spends time socializing and giving affection to the cats.

Although McNamara considers the alpacas easier to care for than the cats, they still take a lot of her time. "They need to be pastured each morning," she says, "fed their hay and grain, and brought into the barn area at night." She removes the dung piles from both field and the barn areas every day and, for the safety of the animals, regularly checks that the fences are secure. She also watches for deer in the fields because they can harbor meningeal worm, which can be deadly to alpacas. Alpaca babies, known as crias, need to be weighed daily, and because they cannot regulate their own body temperature for a while after birth, the barn must be kept warm in the winter.

McNamara acknowledges the truth to the old saying among people who raise animals: "When you deal with livestock, you deal with deadstock." She learned this reality early in her work. "I have many times worked on an animal that was not breathing at birth and got it to breathe, only to have it die a few days later. You have to learn when to intervene and when to let nature take its course." She notes that, while around-the-clock feedings can be very tiring, "the joy you feel when you watch the little ones grow up to be happy and healthy makes it all worth it, despite the sleepless nights, the constant worrying, the moodiness."

Social skills are essential for breeders. "To raise animals, you have to have people skills, a sense of humor, and an ability to judge people over the telephone or through email. You must be able to talk to people easily and make them feel at ease with you." She keeps track of each animal that she has raised, saying, "I believe very strongly in after-sales support: That is critical not only to see how the animals are doing but to also keep track of your breeding program. If any problems crop up that cannot be explained, the animal is pulled from the breeding program. My number one concern is to breed healthy animals." This follow-up is essential, because "if you do not have a good reputation, you have nothing."

Although McNamara gave up a full-time job to be at home with her animals, where she felt she was more needed, she has "constant disruptions" during her days. She has to entertain prospective clients "at all hours of the day" and cannot do many of the things that she would like to do. She has to be well organized, carefully dividing her time between the cats and the alpacas. "At times you need outside help from neighbors, vets, family, and so forth," she adds. "Living in a rural community makes that very easy, as we all share each others' workload whenever it is possible."

Her website is very important in her work since "ninety-five percent of my cats are sold via the Internet." She spends a great deal of time on the telephone and writing emails regarding both types of animals that she breeds. She uses email to answer questions from new breeders and to correspond with other breeders about problems. She also appreciates the speed of email, which has helped her obtain critical health-care information quickly.

McNamara has no formal schooling beyond high school, but, in addition to her years of experience with animals, she has spent "countless hours" reading and researching information about the breeding, care, and health of animals and talking to breeders and farmers. She notes that "when I got the alpacas in 1998, our farmer friend down the road would call when a calf was being born so I could observe and learn about possible complications." She also seeks help from various vets when necessary.

Typical career paths for breeders, McNamara says, include previous experience as a veterinarian, a humane society employee, an animal judge, or a volunteer at shelters or vet clinics. She believes that a science background can also be helpful for breeders. Because hands-on animal experience is so essential, veterinarians and vet technicians really do have a distinct advantage in this type of work. McNamara recommends that individuals who do not have such experience work as a volunteer, whether with a humane society, on a local farm, or in some other capacity.

According to McNamara, the outlook for breeding cats is good. "It is never hard to sell cats. This is horrible to say, but I have chosen a career that will always be in demand. People will always lose deeply loved family pets, and I am there to give them that joy back." The situation is different for alpacas. "If you do not spend the money to market the alpacas, you will have a very difficult time selling them," she says. When the U.S. border closed to ruminants in 2003, Canadian livestock breeders had major problems, and some animals purchased by individuals south of the border could not be imported.

McNamara has lots of advice for would-be breeders. She begins with the obvious: "Research, research, and more research. Knowledge is key—without it you have nothing." McNamara suggests talking to other breeders, determining whether there is a market in your area, and learning about the competition. "With the alpacas," she notes, "there are people who will work the farm with you for free room and board, just for the experience." She suggests that persons who want to get experience this way should leave their name at vet clinics, offering their services. "Doing this will help you decide whether this is the right path for you to take." Another very important consideration is local zoning laws. Prospective breeders need to know whether the law allows them to raise animals in their home or on their property.

The major downside of her chosen career is, says McNamara, "the fact that you lose your social life, since every waking moment is spent thinking, planning, creating, and worrying. Breeding any animal is a full-time job. I bring these animals into this world and am, therefore, responsible for their happiness and well-being. . . . You have no life when you have animals, as they *are* your life."

McNamara also emphasizes that "you do *not* make money breeding cats. You have to do it for the love of the animal. The expenses far outweigh the income you bring in *if* you are doing the proper things like getting vet care when it is needed, providing complete balanced diets, and providing toys that encourage exercise and mental health. You cannot buy a cat and just sit and watch it. They need the human interaction to keep both the mind and body active."

But she is enthusiastic about the things she likes about breeding animals: "There are no words to express the ultimate joy the animals bring to your life, the laughter and the tears." She likes "knowing that you have made a huge difference to a new owner's life, bringing them relief from the sorrow of losing a beloved family pet when it passes. The look on a new pet owner's face when they come and choose that special pet is priceless. . . . That is my ultimate goal, giving something to people that they cannot receive from just anybody."

Profile

PROFESSIONAL DOG TRAINER
Andrea Arden

"Like most dog trainers, I always had a love of dogs and other animals," says Andrea Arden, a professional dog trainer and owner of Andrea Arden Dog Training, a successful dog-training academy in Manhattan. She describes her work this way: "As a professional dog trainer, I teach owners how to teach their dog to be a happy, well-behaved part of their family."

Arden's route to dog training came through experience with her own dog, she says. When she took her dog to a training school, "the school thought I had potential as a dog trainer so they asked me to apprentice with them. After two years I started teaching private lessons and then my own group classes." Later Arden was hired as an on-air trainer for a television show. "I eventually started training my own apprentices," she says, "and developed a staff of trainers who teach group classes and private lessons for my school."

Andrea Arden Dog Training offers varied types of instruction. The private instruction includes one-on-one, daycare, and board training. The latter two help develop socialization skills for dogs that will be placed in daycare or will need to be boarded. The group classes include puppy classes that help to prevent common behavior problems—nipping, chewing, and barking—and provide handling, gentling, and socialization exercises while teaching basic household manners. Adolescent and adult classes give older dogs similar training. Other group classes include agility, tricks, and small-dog basic obedience. The Canine Good Citizen classes are more advanced than basic obedience and include an American Kennel Club certificate for dogs that have successfully completed the classes.

Training dogs is not the only work Arden does, although it is the main focus of most of her other work. She has written four books, three about training dogs and one about traveling with a pet. Arden also writes columns and articles on dog behavior for *Dog Fancy* and other dog magazines and is a member of the Dog Writers Association of America. She has also served on the board of directors of the Association of Pet Dog Trainers and is a Certified Pet Partners Team evaluator for the Delta Society. Her TV credits include her role as the resident professional trainer and field correspondent for the Emmy Award–winning show *The Pet Department*. She has also appeared on *The Today Show* and *Dateline NBC* as well as CBS News and CNN segments.

Arden's path to dog training is similar to that of other trainers, she says. "Most dog trainers start their career by working with and learning from their own dogs, assisting at shelters, and, in some cases, apprenticing with another trainer." She notes that there are many good seminars and conferences on training dogs and that colleges and universities are offering more courses in animal behavior. (Arden's own degree, however, was a triple major combining English, fine arts, and sociology.)

One of the most important skills for a professional dog trainer is the ability to deal with people, Arden says, "since most of what we do is teach people how to become better trainers for their pet dogs. In addition, it is important to possess confidence and good training skills with animals."

Empathy is another helpful trait for good trainers, says Arden. "It is also important to be confident in your knowledge, since your clients will need to develop a trust in your opinion." People who are teaching group classes will need good speaking skills. To create client lesson plans, good writing skills are essential, as well. And since most trainers work freelance, "it is also important to be disciplined with your time," Arden says.

A typical day for Arden includes answering questions from her clients by both telephone and email. She teaches private lessons during the day and group classes in the evenings. She also spends about an hour a day writing books and articles for magazines.

Her day is not typical of trainers who work independently, however. "Essentially, the makeup of a trainer's day depends on what services they offer," Arden says. "Offering private lessons exclusively throughout the day is very different than juggling private lessons, group classes, and board training."

Arden uses email to correspond with clients and answer their questions and maintains a website that gives information about her business. New technology is of limited importance in her work, she says. "I think dog training is a fairly localized and old-fashioned business in that most of my clients are referred to me by other clients. So I really rely on good customer relations to reach out to more people."

Discussing the future for this career, Arden notes that there are lots of dogs that need training, and the opportunities for trainers will, therefore, be many. But she adds that some localities already have an abundance of trainers, so it may be more difficult to train full-time in those areas. "At its best," she says, "dog training is a business that can bring you a sense of fulfillment and offers a flexible work schedule. However, it is generally not a career someone chooses to make a fortune."

Arden's advice to anyone wanting to become a dog trainer is simple: "Take the time to attend as many training classes as you can with your own dog. Also, assist at shelters and read every dog-training book you can get your hands on."

She notes that most dog trainers work for themselves; not many schools hire trainers. However, if individuals want to get a job working with a training school, she advises that they "attend as many training classes as they can with a school they like. This way they can get to know you, assess your basic skills, and, hopefully, bring you on as part of their team."

Arden works closely with dog owners, and she concedes that the one thing that she dislikes about her work has to do with owners. "I sometimes find it stressful to deal with owners who play the blame game," she says, "blaming the dog, the trainers, or just about anyone else for their dog's behavior rather than simply using that energy to train their dog to do what they want." At the same time, one of the things she enjoys most about her work is "working with owners who are responsible and dedicated to sharing their lives with their dogs."

Profile

DOG SHOW JUDGE AND DOG WRITER
Chris Walkowicz

I've been 'in dogs' for thirty-nine years," says Chris Walkowicz, dog show judge and writer. "My background is simply a dedicated interest in cynology [the study of canines]. I have always enjoyed writing, but didn't put it to use until I joined the dog world."

Walkowicz wears two hats in her work: that of a dog show judge and a writer of dog books and articles. Pet ownership was the catalyst that brought her to this work. After purchasing her first dog she realized that she needed to train it, so she joined a dog club. She became involved with club activities, including editing the newsletter, and then began to show and breed dogs. Judging dogs and writing professionally about them was the logical result of her activities and experiences in the dog world. Although it's hard to separate her two jobs—her work week usually involves both judging and writing—Walkowicz talks first about judging.

"The best way to prepare for judging is by owning, breeding, and showing dogs," she says. "The only way to become a dog show judge is experience, years and years of experience in the world of dogs. The minimum requirement is twelve years in the sport, in addition to various other requirements." She advises aspiring judges to begin "cultivating and talking to long-term, quality mentors." She also recommends keeping "complete records of large shows watched, breeds shown, breeds bred, sanctioned matches judged, stewarding assignments, and any other education efforts." Judges need to know the breed standard, and this comes through a "study of the breed—its form and function—gained by attending shows, observing under longtime judges, being mentored, and attending seminars and institutes on the various breeds."

Experience and knowledge are the basic qualification factors for judges. Other important qualifications that Walkowicz cites are "the ability to judge in all sorts of weather and conditions and at all sorts of locales." Judges must be in good health and be able to stand "for several hours and several days in a row." Judges should enjoy or at least tolerate traveling, as they need to do so in the course of their job, sometimes over long distances. She adds, "it is said that the best judges have an eye for the ideal. Of course, we all think we do."

After qualifying as a judge, she says, "we sit back and wait for invitations, because we cannot solicit assignments." One way to help in getting assignments "is to keep your face out and about in the dog world, showing, breeding, doing matches, chatting on lists, participating in club activities, and so on."

Walkowicz is approved to judge all breeds in the herding and working groups, miscellaneous, best in show, and junior showmanship. She is currently working to expand her credentials to judge additional breeds by taking seminars and attending institutes; this takes up some weekends and an entire week in the summer.

Walkowicz travels the country, and sometimes the world, in her judging. Kennel clubs ask her anywhere from five months to two years in advance to judge their shows. In her judging she uses AKC standards or, when in a foreign country, the standards of the local kennel club. She normally judges about two weekends a month, which often means four days of travel and four days of judging per month.

One of the things she enjoys most about judging is the mental workout—comparing the "characteristics of one dog to another and all to the standard." In the process of judging, she notes that "it helps to be, or at least act, confident and to not be thin-skinned." The only things she admits to disliking about judging work are some traveling hassles, such as poor weather, and also the substandard conditions of some show venues.

Walkowicz sees a good future for dog judging: "There are always calls for good, fair judges," she notes. She adds that the chances of getting judging jobs are improved considerably when people are approved for judging more breeds: "All-breed judges are busy every weekend."

The same wealth of experience with dogs strengthens her writing. She is president emeritus of the Dog Writers Association of America (DWAA) and turns out a monthly column about writing for the organization. Although virtually all of her writing is about dogs, Walkowicz is also a member of the Cat Writers Association and has published in cat magazines (and she admits to owning a cat).

Walkowicz has to her credit numerous award-winning articles in magazines and newspapers and online. She published the first of her eight books about dogs in 1985. Her books have been selected for the Book of the Month Club and have won awards such as the DWAA "Best Book of 1985," the American Library Association's Top Reference Book, and the National League of American Pen Women's Best Nonfiction Book. Walkowicz herself received a Dog Writers Association of America Distinguished Service Award for extraordinary achievement and communications excellence in 1995, and she is a former FIDO Woman of the Year. (The FIDO awards, before being discontinued, were among the most prestigious honors given in the dog world.)

Walkowicz emphasizes that writers need to know the basics: "Knowledge of the subject and of grammar, knowledge of the particular audience, and knowledge of the periodical or publishing house." Other essential skills for writers are the ability to interview and research: she considers creative writing courses an asset in developing writing skills. She adds that she wishes now that she had "continued my education to take more courses in literature and to major in English—and perhaps animal husbandry."

Walkowicz enjoys her writing, considering it both a teaching tool and a way to advise others "how to avoid my mistakes." This latter is important to her, because "when we make a mistake, a living creature can suffer." She also enjoys "matching people to the right dog for them and their lifestyles." A fun part of her writing is, she says, "evoking emotions—trying to induce someone to laugh or to experience poignancy or goosebumps that can only come through the love of a dog."

The negatives about writing are easy for her to list. "Waiting, sometimes a ridiculous amount of time, for payment" and "the length of time between creation and publication" are her main annoyances. Writers also need to have a "thick skin to let the rejections and criticisms roll off your back," she concedes. However, she finds that all of this is easily compensated for by the thrill of "seeing your name as a byline or on the cover of a book. It is an act of creation just short of giving birth!"

Her advice to would-be writers is simply: "Write. Join a local writing organization and a critiquing group. Take creative writing courses. Volunteer to write for organizations' newsletters." In terms of dog writing, "the better writers have a passion for their subject. So it's good to have or interact with dogs." She notes that a good way to get writing jobs is to develop an expertise in a certain field, whether through education or experience. Would-be writers can also write "gratis pieces, such as for newsletters or clubs, to gain experience and build credits." It's important to keep track of all published work through what is known as a "credit sheet." Walkowicz notes that it is becoming harder to break into the publishing field. Good credentials, such as experience and past writing accomplishments, help to successfully pitch an article or a book. But "even those with credits still have to work harder to make a sale."

Walkowicz is not currently working on a nine-to-five basis, but her schedule is very busy with involvement in two clubs, judging duties, and other related activities. She also has various duties associated with her position of judges education chair for the Bearded Collie Club of America, including traveling to make presentations on the breed. In between all of her activities, she answers emails and takes care of paperwork and club matters. Any spare moments are devoted to collating an anthology of her columns and developing another book.

Walkowicz notes that before her involvement with the DWAA and the Bearded Collie Club, her days were considerably less cluttered and more structured. "I usually wrote for one half day," she says, "doing paperwork and email in the afternoon, with local shows on the weekends."

Ultimately, Walkowicz's love for both judging and writing is obvious: "I spend just about every day with animals except when traveling," she enthuses.

Chapter 3

Horses

History was written on the back of the horse.
inscription at The Horse Park
in Lexington, Kentucky

The horse was domesticated by humans some five thousand years ago in Eurasia, in what is now eastern Ukraine, central Russia, and Kazakhstan. Horses were initially raised for food and milk. Later, humans used their speed and maneuverability in war and for travel. As time went by, new breeds and advances in equipment made the horse even more indispensable to civilization: heavy draft horses were better for farming than lighter horses, shoulder collar harnesses made plowing more efficient, and the stirrup gave soldiers new battle capabilities. For a very long time, the horse was the main means of transportation and communication.

In developed countries today, horses are used for leisure and sports. Riding for pleasure is becoming increasingly widespread, and the types of shows and show events for horses continue to increase. Horse racing—whether harness racing with the horse pulling a small cart (the "sulky") and driver, or the more familiar variety with the jockey astride a standard-bred horse—remains very popular. More than two hundred breeds of horses are now recognized, and rodeos and events aimed at specific breeds are becoming more common.

The fact that a great deal of money is spent on pursuits relating to horses is not surprising. A poll by the Horse Industry Alliance taken in 2000 reported that more money was being spent on horses than was being spent by the movie industry. Because of this and the many job opportunities available, publications often write about work related to horses in a separate horse industry section. Jobs range from hands-on work, such as training horses or teaching riding, to jobs that actually involve little or no contact with horses. In many respects, they are similar to work with other animals. Many are not full-time, but several can be creatively combined to provide fulltime work.

Patrick Evans, Manager of the Nepean National Equestrian Park in Nepean, Canada, says: "Work with horses is a very physical career. You need to be able to embrace the way the horse industry works—be able to get up in the early morning after working late at night, and enjoy getting up early. You need to have high energy and patience and be physically fit."

In his career, Evans has followed the advice given by a mentor in his two-year equine studies course: "Work in as many different parts of the horse industry as possible, and work for 'great people.'" He adds, "Humility is important in the horse industry. Even with my diploma, I started out on the bottom and worked my way up as they saw what I could do."

Sarah Mayo—who trains horses, runs day camps for riders, and is an experienced instructor—calls working with horses a "passion, a labor of love. You must love being outdoors and being with horses." Julie Cull, media relations coordinator for Equine Canada, Canada's national horse organization, agrees. "Don't choose a career with horses without the passion," she says. "You do it for the love, and then it becomes a career."

AN OVERVIEW OF HORSE-RELATED JOBS

Because of the size of the horse industry, it supports a large number of varied jobs. The following overview is designed to give a general survey of occupations that are at least partially related to horses. It is based on information developed by Equine Canada to help answer the numerous employment questions that they receive.

For many of these jobs, nothing in the actual nature of the job necessarily relates to horses. Accounting, for example, involves working with money and keeping records. All organizations or businesses that deal with horses—such as large breeding farms and show or racing venues—have jobs for accountants, and an accountant who loves horses may especially enjoy working for such an employer. On the other hand, occupations such as breeding involve extensive direct contact with horses. Many of these more hands-on jobs are covered in more detail later in the chapter.

Business Services
Business services relate to the operation and financial management of any organization or business. People working in business services within the horse industry may have little direct contact with horses, but their knowledge of and interest in them can be an asset. They may even receive attractive perks, such as tickets to horse events.

Some of the work with business services includes jobs for accountants and bookkeepers; appraisers; auctioneers; business, finance, and marketing consultants; insurance salespeople, investigators, and providers; lawyers; sales agents; auditors; and travel operators. These business services are needed for racetracks, horse parks, horse shows, rodeos, breeding farms, individual breeders, and associations.

Education
With the growth of the horse industry has come additional educational programs and expansion in existing programs. Teachers and support staff are needed at colleges and universities with equine studies programs as well as vocational and training schools, some of which are run by prominent horse trainers. Writers provide instructional material for classroom use, and, in some areas, county agricultural or extension agents help to educate students.

Farm or Barn Facilities
The facilities needed for horses include riding arenas, barns, carriages, fencing, and stalls. People designing this equipment must know how much space is needed, and the manufacturer must know the best materials for the type of wear that comes from horses using the equipment. Individuals with a good knowledge of horses will have an advantage in designing and selling these products. The jobs available in this area include equipment design, which is sometimes done by an architect; manufacturing; carpentry and painting; and distribution and retailing.

Health Care
Primary health care for horses comes from veterinarians; other individuals provide therapies such as chiropractic, acupuncture, and massage. Information on veterinary work and most therapies is covered in Chapter 10. For equine massage, see page 63.

Other people essential for horse health are farriers, who shoe horses, and grooms, who provide daily care. Additionally, manufacturers, distributors, and retailers of drugs, feed, and supplements may employ equine nutrition consultants, pharmaceutical sales representatives, and other individuals who get to work with horses.

Equipment

Equipment that is used in training, driving, and riding horses demands a great deal of knowledge. This equipment includes saddles, bridles, horse carts, and cart harnesses, all of which provide work for designers, manufacturers, distributors, and retailers. A different set of people work with equipment intended for humans (including protective headgear), clothing (such as jodhpurs, boots, and jockey silks), and gift items. Additionally, individuals who repair leather equipment must understand how it is used and the pressures to which it is subjected.

Organizations and Associations

Horse-related organizations and youth clubs operate on national and state/provincial levels—these include U.S.A. Equestrian, Equine Canada, and the American Youth Horse Council. Of the more than two hundred horse breeds recognized, at least twenty-five have their own associations, as do some major sports—such as jumping and dressage. These groups offer jobs such as president or organization head, media relations coordinator, membership chair, auditor, and business or accounting staff. Other positions can include coordinators who work with representatives of the different breeds or events, a communications director in charge of publications and member communications, and journalists who write for these publications.

Professionals

In most cases, professionals are considered to be those individuals who have been trained for direct work with horses. Professionals in the horse industry include horse breeders; large breeding establishments have specialized positions such as breeding farm manager, bloodstock agent, artificial inseminator, stallion manager, broodmare manager, and foaling attendant. Other professionals are trainers, riding instructors, riding coaches, and grooms. These jobs are covered later in this chapter.

Stables
Stables board horses and give riding lessons, and some have riding camps. In addition to the owners and operators, jobs in stables include horse grooms and riding teachers. These are also covered later in the chapter.

Horse Shows and Racing Facilities
These facilities may have management positions such as racetrack administrator available. They may also need guards, grounds maintenance staff, track maintenance staff, publicity staff, stewards, horse show judges, a clocker, track superintendent, paddock judge, a stable manager, an exercise rider, and mutuel staff (who are involved with on-track betting). Other work during events are those often found in sports venues: concession operators, ticket sellers, parking attendants, and so forth. Additional information on horse shows is provided later in the chapter.

Recreation
Recreational activity is growing steadily within the horse industry as more people ride for pleasure. This category includes positions such as park and recreation administrator, recreation planner, trail engineer, packer and guide, trail crew member, and reservation clerk.

Creative Work
There are various opportunities for applying creative talent to work with horses. Artists and photographers use their knowledge of horses, especially horse conformation, to develop or create pictures of horses that are flattering. Publishers of horse-related magazines and books need a good knowledge of horses, and writers who write for these horse magazines or write horse books need knowledge about horses. Web designers who are knowledgeable about horses will know the best way to present the industry and the most useful links for websites.

Other
Other types of work are as varied as stunt rider and film editor. There are also many positions that are more a labor of love than an actual paying job, horse rescue worker and horse sanctuary owner among them.

HORSE SHOW WORK

Salary Range: As with other horse work, salaries vary greatly, from around $10,000 to $55,000 with a median of $27,000.

Educational Requirements: Years of experience with horses, some courses, and apprenticing.

Employment Outlook: As shows continue to increase in number and type, so will jobs.

Horse shows are categorized as either Western or English. The most basic distinguishing feature of the two categories is saddle design: Western saddles have a horn and English saddles do not. However, within these two categories are many different styles of saddles, with the exact design depending on the type of competition for which it is intended. For example, Western saddles for cutting events are different from those used in roping events. In English riding a different saddle is used for each event. A recent Horse Industry Alliance poll reported that eighty percent of the households with people who ride favored Western.

Western riding comes from the "Old West," when cowboys depended on horses in their work on cattle ranches and on cattle drives. Today, these work skills are competitions and are popular worldwide. Divisions in Western shows include cutting, reining, general performance, and speed. Rodeos, with many different events for horses, are another part of the Western tradition, as are the controversial chuck wagon races, which often include horse injuries or fatalities.

The types of English horse shows include dressage, cross-country, stadium jumping, hunter jumping, endurance, vaulting, and three-day eventing. In dressage, riders are judged on their ability to communicate instructions to the horse for a set pattern of turns around the ring. In cross-country shows, the course contains jumps and different types of terrain, and the ability of the rider to guide the horse over the course is the crucial factor. Stadium jumping, perhaps the most well-known of these shows, has a set number of jumps, and the rider must guide the horse over the jumps with a minimal number of errors and within a certain time limit. In the show ring, horses entered in the hunter class are judged on gait, style, and the ability to clear the jumps. In endurance competitions, the horse and rider travel a set distance—usually a hundred miles—at high speed along a cross-country track; this tests the horse's speed and endurance and the rider's knowledge of pacing and use of the horse. Vaulting essentially consists of doing gymnastics on horseback and includes individual, pair, and team competitions. Three-day eventing includes dressage, jumping, cross-country, and endurance, with a different focus on each of the three days.

Horse Show Officials

Different officials, many of them volunteers, keep a horse show running smoothly. The number and types of positions depend on the size, level, and type of show. Smaller, local shows will not have as many different officials as larger shows, where there may be more specialized roles.

At the top is the show manager, who handles overall show administration—planning, organizing, and hiring officials for each show. The show secretary keeps track of show entries and other show details. Larger shows have an in-gate attendant to keep the riders and horses on schedule for their appearances and a ringmaster to enforce discipline if needed. The course designer designs the course layout and a jump crew helps the course designer move the fences, as necessary, during the show. The timekeeper handles the time system, whether it is automatic or by hand. The announcer keeps competitors and public alike informed, and a horse show veterinarian is on hand for all shows.

Horse Show Judge

Of the jobs at horse shows, professional horse show judges are the most prestigious and rewarding, but also the most demanding in terms of time and stamina. They rank horses in a show following the criteria developed by a breed organization or the governing organization of the show.

The two basic categories of horse judging are conformation and performance. Conformation simply means the physical attributes of a horse, and conformation requirements are different for each breed. For example, good muscle development is an essential attribute of the Tennessee Walking Horse; muscling allows Tennessee Walkers to produce the trademark smooth gait. Judges must be able recognize correct balance, method of movement, and structure. Performance judging looks at how the horse performs while being ridden.

Horse judges follow the requirements laid out by the association that sanctions a show. Each association, such as U.S.A. Equestrian, has specifications for licensing judges. Judging positions in the large horse shows pay well, and some few judges work full-time going to different shows around the world. Most work on a part-time basis, however.

A judge needs to be expert with and have a good eye for horses and have many years' experience in the horse industry. Horse show judges usually spend a number of years studying and perfecting the evaluation of horses. Some associations require judges to be licensed, take specialized training, or attend certain clinics and courses.

Technical Delegate (Steward)

The immediate role of technical delegates, or stewards, is to prevent cheating and abuse of horses in shows. Essentially, they ensure the safety of the horses, the riders, and the spectators by looking after countless small details. Pay for technical delegates is not high. This work is done for the love of the sport.

The work of technical delegates begins several months before the actual competition when they receive the list of events. At that point, they check carefully to verify that judges are qualified for their jobs and to ensure that a vet is on call and that appropriate human medical assistance is available. During the show they stay in close contact with the organizers. They usually arrive quite early on the day of the show, or the day before, and may stay quite late. Responsibilities on show day include ensuring that the course builder created the jumps correctly and that no cheating or cruelty takes place in the practice arena. During a show there must be no conversation between competitors and judges. If the competitors disagree with the decision of the judge they talk to the technical delegate, who serves as a go-between to the judge. In dressage, the technical delegate checks for the use of illegal equipment or the illegal use of legal equipment. Bits, spurs, and whips can be strictly regulated or prohibited altogether, depending on the class. The judge's booth must be in the correct position and the letters on the dressage arena correctly placed.

Christine Hickman of Dunrobin, Ontario, has been a steward for seventeen years. "Stewarding enables horse shows to run," she says. "We're really there to make it fair to everyone."

Hickman's lifelong experience with horses began in her childhood. She has competed in show jumping, eventing, and dressage (now her specialty as a steward), although she competed at a fairly low level and not in national championships. Hickman has also bred horses, and her children have competed.

Hickman gave up working directly with horses for health reasons and has found stewarding a way to stay involved with horses. "Horses are not a cheap hobby," she says. "But they are a very rewarding hobby." Additionally, Hickman runs a consignment tack shop and she teaches courses for prospective stewards.

A steward is "there to help people, not to 'catch' them doing something illegal," Hickman says. As a steward for dressage, she works with both horses and riders, checking them when they enter and leave the ring. She needs a good rapport with the judge and show organizers. She also has to deal with competitive parents and coaches as well as excited and nervous competitors. "It's a wonderful job until something goes wrong," she says. "It can have nasty moments. The steward may not be popular with people." She adds that an essential quality a steward must have is diplomacy, especially when something goes wrong. Stewards must find the right time to talk to someone who is not following the rules (not when others are around, for example) and the right way to do it (not too loudly).

HORSE CARE
Salary Range: $10,000 to more than $55,000; median salary is $27,000.
Educational Requirements: No requirements, although animal science and equine studies are helpful.
Employment Outlook: As the use of horses for leisure grows, these jobs will remain steady and may increase.

Groom
Horse grooms work daily with horses. Although the exact content of a groom's work depends upon many factors, including his or her personal skills and the expectations and size of the employer's barn, the following tasks are typical of a groom's work.

Grooms feed and water horses, ensure that they are eating, watch for signs of illness, and care for sick animals. They also exercise horses, which includes, when necessary, oiling their feet beforehand and grooming them afterward, while their pores are still open. Grooms sometimes clean the stalls (known as "mucking out") and spread new bedding on the floors ("bedding down"). Many grooms clean the saddles and bridles of the horses for which they are responsible. Harness horse grooms must clean all of the reins and the harness used by these horses in racing. Additionally, they take care of the horse's legs, often rubbing them with various liniments and wrapping them for travel as necessary.

Grooms must be dedicated to horses and genuinely care for them. They must be skilled with their hands, have good personal stamina, exhibit good communication skills, and be observant and responsible. The only required background for this work is some knowledge of horses and the ability to ride. Working as a groom often serves as an entry-level position for work with horses. It is an excellent, hands-on way to learn about horse care. Grooms may progress to other jobs as their skills and knowledge increase. Sometimes riders take part-time work as grooms to help pay for riding lessons.

Horse grooms find work in riding schools, stables, breeding farms, and competition stables. Some employers in large stables have a promotion path that leads to the position of head groom, or grooms may be promoted to stable manager. Companies that specialize in transporting horses by air to competitions often provide a horse groom or grooms for the duration of the flight to ensure good care and attention to the horses while in transit.

Grooms often live at the establishment where they work and travel with horses to different competitions. Most of their work is outdoors, in all types of weather, or in stables, which may not be entirely clean and fresh. Salaries vary tremendously and depend on the employer. They may include room and board and even the cost of any necessary training. Grooms often work long hours, especially during the busy competition season.

Farrier (Blacksmith)

A farrier, popularly known as a blacksmith, is responsible for maintaining a horse's hooves and making horseshoes to fit each horse. Farriers visit a horse regularly to maintain the hooves, which may involve resetting the shoes, putting on new shoes, or installing a pad. To do the job well a farrier needs to know horse anatomy and physiology and apply this knowledge to an individual horse's gait. Expert hoof trimming and horseshoes that fit well are very important aspects of a horse's performance in the show ring, on the racetrack, in other sports, and in pleasure riding.

A farrier needs to have physical strength, especially in the arms and back. Certification from an accredited school is required; this usually involves a full-time, six-week course. An apprenticeship with an experienced farrier is recommended. Although a background with horses is not necessary for farriers, it is useful in helping them spot problems with the way a horse moves.

EQUINE MASSAGE THERAPY

Salary Range: Varies greatly; many practitioners massage part-time and have earnings from other therapeutic jobs.

Educational Requirements: Technical training is required, but the profession is unregulated. Certificates from institutions indicate only that a course was completed.

Employment Outlook: This is a growing occupation, but the demand is not yet stable.

Equine Sports Massage Therapy (ESMT), or massage for horses, is generally viewed as a fairly recent phenomenon. It is not new, however: thousands of years ago, the Greeks had the practice of massaging both horses and warriors before they went to battle. Today, along with other therapies, ESMT is being used more and more to treat horses, which are athletes in their own right. The horse is, in essence, a motion machine, and the musculoskeletal system is mainly responsible for producing that motion. (In fact, in horses the musculoskeletal system is the largest part of their bodies—some sixty percent.) As with human athletes, the very process of training and using the muscles makes them vulnerable to strain and spasm. This is where ESMT comes in.

ESMT aims to keep the muscles functioning well, or to assist in situations where there has been muscle injury. Essentially, it is the therapeutic manipulation of soft body tissues, mainly muscles, that benefits the nervous, muscular, and circulatory systems. It is distinct from veterinary work, and ESMTs emphasize that their work is not a substitute for veterinary work. In fact, in England a law was passed in 1966 that therapies such as massage or aromatherapy cannot be used without the permission of a veterinarian. Further, these therapists are not allowed to diagnose—only a veterinarian can do that.

ESMT is more common in Europe, the United Kingdom, Canada, Asia, and Pacific Rim countries than in the United States. The use of ESMT in the United States is usually considered to have begun in the 1970s when Jack Meagher, known for treating National Football League players, was asked to treat the U.S. equine team. Meagher used his equine massage skills (known as the Meagher Method) on the U.S. team in the 1976 Olympics; they subsequently won the gold medal. The Meagher Method remains the standard ESMT procedure, and other methods are weighed against it. ESMT is now an integral part of the U.S. Olympic equestrian team and for horse racing in general.

Because of the unregulated nature of the profession, people who want to enter it should do so with a fair degree of caution, obtaining as much information as possible. People already practicing ESMT are a good source of information; it is advisable to consult with several therapists, as one individual may be highly idiosyncratic. Institutions offering courses in ESMT include the British Columbia College of Equine Therapy in Canada, the Australian College of Animal Tactile Therapy, and the Western Montana School of Equine Massage. Many individuals and smaller institutions also teach ESMT. Prospective students are advised to investigate thoroughly any training institution, examining the training and experience of the teachers in particular.

For information on other alternative therapies, see Chapter 10.

HORSE TRAINING

Salary Range: $10,000 to more than $55,000. The median salary is $27,000. Trainers of winning racehorses will earn more.

Educational Requirements: Long experience with horses; courses in equine studies and life sciences are an asset.

Employment Outlook: There will always be work for good horse trainers.

Trainer

A horse trainer ensures that a horse can be ridden or driven and will follow rider or driver commands. Cowboy movies and books about the U.S. and Canadian West popularized a method of training horses for riding known as "breaking" a horse—essentially, breaking a horse's will to resist the intrusion of a rider and equipment on its head and back. The method brought to general public attention through the book and movie *The Horse Whisperer* is a gentler method of training, often called "natural horse training," that seeks to change the horses' response to being ridden, driven, and trained by humans to one of cooperation. Although some consider this approach to training a recent phenomenon, horse aficionados say that the gentler method is much older than is popularly believed. People in the forefront of natural horse training today include Monty Roberts, Frank Bell, Pat Parelli, Carolyn Resnick, John Lyons, Richard Shrake, Pony Boy, and Clint Anderson. Roberts operates a certification program that is taught worldwide and headquartered at Flag Is Up Farms in Solvang, California.

Horse trainers usually specialize in a specific type of horse. They train thoroughbred horses for horse races; standard-bred horses for pulling a sulky in pacing or trotting races; performance horses for eventing, show jumping, and dressage; Western event horses; and horses that are ridden solely for pleasure. Essentially, the horses used in the race and show events are athletes, and trainers are responsible for improving their stamina and the other qualities necessary for excelling in these settings. On the job, the trainer is also responsible for getting the horses used to reins, saddles, and harnesses.

Very skilled horse trainers may give horse training clinics for juniors, amateurs, and other trainers. Trainers in a small operation may also work as riding instructors or riders. Trainers at a large horse farm may ride in horse show classes early in the week, leaving the owners to ride their horses in the final events at the end of the week.

Riding Instructor

Riding instructors teach clients basic riding techniques, including the correct way to mount a horse, the correct position for riding, and how to post, or ride well, the different gaits of a horse. Their clients can range from professionals to rank amateurs, and instructors must be able to determine the skill level of their pupils and help them in the areas where they are weak. Instructors may also teach children how to ride.

In addition to being skilled with people, riding instructors must be physically fit and good riders, at the very least up to the level being taught. They need to have patience and be able to calm nervous students. They must have good communications skills and enthusiasm to motivate their pupils while maintaining discipline, and they need to be well-organized to provide a training program for all levels of pupils and ensure that students are in top physical and mental form. The instructional program they develop needs to be practical at the same time that it provides a good foundation for students who may go on to become professional riders. Instructors also need to carefully monitor student progress so that training changes as necessary to maximize developing riding skills. The very fact that horses are large, powerful animals means that horseback riding can be dangerous; riding instructors are responsible for the safety of their students at all times.

The qualifications of riding instructors are not controlled by any governmental body, but the horse industry has provided its own regulation. The American Riding Instructors Association (ARIA) was established in 1984 with the aim of promoting instruction in a safe, knowledgeable, and professional manner. The ARIA certification program is an attempt to bring high standards to a basically unregulated profession. Instructors certified through the American Riding Instructors Certification Program (ARICP) are listed on the national ARICP website, and their qualifications are recognized throughout the United States. In England, qualifications come through the British Horse Society or the Association of British Riding Schools.

In some establishments, the riding instructor also trains horses, but at others the two functions are separate. Riding instructors are usually given a certain number of horses to care for, and they must at least ensure that the horses they use in their training are well-trained and obedient. The usual work setting is outdoors, no matter what the weather is like. Some may use an indoor arena, but this is the exception rather than the rule. Riding instructors may also need to travel, especially if they are instructing or coaching professional riders.

Riding instructors often work long hours, and pay, although there is some variation, can be fairly good. Self-employed instructors need a certain amount of business sense. In some settings, the work may be seasonal, but instructors can find year-round work in riding schools, private stables, and stables at schools that offer equine courses. At competition stables, the instructors work with horses used in show jumping and eventing, and this work may require travel. Some tourist companies or organizations offer vacations on horseback that include trail riding, often only on a seasonal basis; these companies generally need to have riding instructors on staff. Many instructors also ride competitively.

With the increasing popularity of horse riding, the prospects in this field are good. Beginning instructors may be able to look forward to a promotion to head riding instructor, a position in a large riding stable, or work as a judge in competitions.

See profile on page 72.

Horse Rider

Horse riders ride horses in shows or competitions. They are sometimes known as "equestrians," which simply means they are skilled in riding horses. The term refers to both male and female riders. An "equestrienne," however, is a female skilled in riding horses.

Most riders ride horses in shows for the love of riding, not for money. These are the people who compete in local horse shows, where the level of competition may not be as high as in the national and international competitions. They will earn some money when they win, but it is not a significant income. However, the top riders at horse shows and rodeos are often well paid. Few riders at horse shows ride on a full-time basis, as much because of the scheduling of shows as the low pay. Many of the top riders also train other riders, who work with them in a kind of apprenticeship. Others own stables that board horses and provide riding lessons. They may also train horses.

Professional riders include the jockeys who race thoroughbred horses. Jockeys need to be small (to meet weight requirements) and strong, and they must have a good understanding of horses—especially the horse that they ride in each race. Jockeys who ride the top horses can earn a substantial income, but most make somewhere between $6,000 and $25,000 a year.

Although they don't sit astride a horse, sulky riders in harness races have to guide the horse skillfully on the track and, hopefully, to a win. Again, these riders need to be small, knowledgeable about horses, and skilled in threading their way down a track. As with jockeys, sulky riders who guide the top horses earn a good income, but most others earn much less.

Additional trainer information on pages 12, 84, 88, and 101.

HORSE BUSINESS

Salary Range: Overall, similar to other work with horses (between $10,000 to more than $55,000), but subject to greater variation. A breeder's salary depends on the market, while an appraiser's can range from $30,000 to $80,000.

Educational Requirements: Experience with horses essential; equine and life sciences courses an asset.

Employment Outlook: Appraising is a growing field with great opportunities. The market for breeders is steady to good.

Horse Breeder

Horse breeders raise horses to sell to people who want to compete in horse shows or horse races or who simply want to have a horse for pleasure riding. Some breeders work in a facility that also offers boarding and riding instruction. Many, however, are only involved in the business of raising and selling foals (young horses) for sale.

Horse breeders must know about different bloodlines of horses to select a sire (father) and dam (mother) who have complementary pedigrees. Depending upon the purpose for which the horse is being bred, the breeder will look for different traits. With race horses, for instance, a sire with good physical conformation and speed may be bred to a dam with a bloodline containing many previous winners.

Positions at a large horse breeding establishment include general manager, broodmare manager, and stallion manager. There may also be work for grooms and, depending upon the size of the establishment, trainers and riding instructors.

At larger establishments, the general manager oversees the total operation, dealing with farm maintenance, managing staff, and taking care of all business and financial dealings. He or she is also responsible for customer relations. At smaller establishments, the general manager may do the work of broodmare and stallion managers; otherwise, they report to the general manager.

A broodmare manager is in charge of all aspects of the care and maintenance of mares and foals. This individual generally works closely with both the farm manager and veterinarian. Of primary importance is ensuring that mares are healthy. Nutrition is becoming increasingly important in maintaining the reproductive efficiency and health of broodmares. The broodmare manager oversees nutrition programs designed for each individual mare in consultation with equine nutrition experts.

The stallion manager takes care of the stallions, ensuring that they are in top condition and ready for breeding. Because reproductive success often depends on the stallion, the stallion manager works to identify potential problems and, if possible, correct them. A breeding stallion cannot breed more than forty-five or so mares during the short breeding season, however; artificial insemination (AI) is increasingly being used for breeding (except in the case of thoroughbreds for racing, where it is not allowed). In the AI program, the stallion manager is responsible for providing high-quality semen at the proper time for the mares to be bred. To do this, the manager needs to continually monitor the stallions to improve their production of usable semen. He or she must also oversee the processing and shipping of the semen. During this entire process, the stallion manager must pay careful attention to detail and coordinate carefully with the broodmare manager or owner and a veterinarian.

Equine Appraiser

Equine appraisal is a growing field whose members are increasingly accorded the status of professionals. It is open to all qualified horse people. Some equine appraisers specialize in a particular breed or type of horse, gaining a reputation for their detailed knowledge of the breed. Others appraise all horses, accepting the diversity as a professional challenge.

Downturns in the economy that influence horse prices can affect the work of trainers and breeders, but appraising is generally little affected by such changes. Although fewer sales are made during these times, appraisals are still needed, and the field is generally more stable than other types of work involving horses.

Horses must be appraised objectively, with no regard for personal likes or dislikes. The field is becoming more challenging as horse buyers and sellers gain a greater knowledge of horses and more people enter the horse business as an investment. Equine appraisers must provide accurate information to these individuals to help them make wise investments.

In addition to assisting with investment decisions, horse appraisals are needed by lawyers for divorce and estate settlements. Appraisals are also used in cases of bankruptcies and by insurance companies in setting insurance rates. They are important for partnership details, estate and tax planning, organizing or changing family trusts, and appraising real estate. The services of equine appraisers are used by accountants, banks, breed associations, government agencies, lawyers, real estate appraisers, and realtors.

The American Society of Equine Appraisers has been working to elevate horse appraisal work to professional status and to support its membership. This support is essential for individuals who are beginning to work in appraising. As mentioned, the field is growing with opportunities in most areas of the United States. Pay for an experienced equine appraiser is quite good, roughly equivalent to that of an architect or accountant. An average annual salary is $47,000, with the range from about $30,300 to $80,000 a year.

RESOURCES

American Farriers Association
4059 Iron Works Parkway, Suite 1
Lexington, KY 40511
phone: 859-233-7411
fax: 859-231-7862
email: farriers@americanfarriers.org
www.americanfarriers.org

American Horse Racing Federation
1700 K Street, NW
Washington, DC 20006
phone: 202-296-4031
fax: 202-296-1970

American Riding Instructors Association (ARIA)
28801 Trenton Court
Bonita Springs, FL 34134-3337
phone: 239-948-3232
fax: 239-948-5053
email: riding-instructor@comcast.net
www.riding-instructor.com

American Society of Equine Appraisers (ASEA)
1126 Eastland Drive N, Suite 100
P.O. Box 186
Twin Falls, ID 83303-0186
phone: 800-704-7020
fax: 208-733-2326
email: equine@equineappraiser.com
www.equineappraiser.com

American Youth Horse Council
577 North Boyero Avenue
Pueblo West, CO 81007
phone: 800-879-2942
fax: 775-256-0382
email: info@ayhc.com
www.ayhc.org

Association of British Riding Schools
Queen's Chambers
38-40 Queen Street
Penzance, Cornwall
phone: 01736-369440
fax: 01736-351390
England TR18 4BH

The British Horse Society
Stoneleigh Deer Park
Kenilworth, Warwickshire
England CV8 2XZ
phone: 01926-707700
fax: 01926-707800
www.bhs.org.uk

Canadian Horse Breeders Association (CHBA)
5, Rang 3 Gravel
Ferme Neuve, QC
Canada J0W 1CO
phone: 819-587-4321
email: secc@sympatico.ca
www.chevalcanadien.com

Equine Canada/Canada Hippique
2460 Lancaster Road
Ottawa, Ontario
Canada K1B 4S5
phone: 613-248-3433
fax: 613-248-3484
www.equinecanada.ca

Sport Horse Owners and Breeders Association
PMB 241
6753 Thomasville Road, Suite 108
Tallahassee, FL 32312
phone: 850-893-8532
fax: 850-893-8954
email: soba@sport-horse.org
www.sport-horse.org

United States Equestrian Federation
4047 Iron Works Parkway
Lexington, KY 40511
phone: 859-258-2472
fax: 859-231-6662
www.usef.org

Job Listings and Web Information

Information on all aspects of horses, including services and breeds, is available at www.knowledgehorse.com/services

Equimax
Described as "The Leading Horse Industry Employment Service Since 1986," this site has information for both job seekers and employers: www.equimax.com.

Mary K. Employment Service, Ocala, FL
Temporary and permanent job placement service in the horse industry. Some temporary positions may become permanent after some time of satisfactory service: www.equistaff.com.

Professional Equine Employment Management
This employment agency specializes in jobs in the horse industry: www.equinepros.com or 800-733-6008.

Profile

HEAD INSTRUCTOR
Anna Twinney

Before Anna Twinney began her career with horses, she worked for the Leicestershire Constabulary in England, with duties that included investigative interview training, investigations of multicultural crime and major incidents (including drug and surveillance), investigations of rape and child victims, and review of the constabulary itself. After enjoying a week's vacation at a working cattle ranch in Wyoming and Montana, she found herself wondering "why some people could live in a place they loved, doing exactly what their heart told them to do, and I wasn't supposed to be one of them. The response I received when I got home was: 'That's what vacations are for.' "

A wonderful vacation in Jamaica the next year brought up the same question again: "Why should I wake up every day to grey garages and be abused by people who could not understand that we were trying to make a positive impact on their lives?"

So she decided to make a change. "When I began this journey," says Twinney, "my dream was to find inner peace—to find a place where I could wake up every morning and feel that I was in paradise. To want to get up in the morning and feel that every day was a blessing—to see and be in nature."

As her dream evolved it began to focus on horses. She had ridden horses as a child, and in her free time away from the constabulary, she rode her thoroughbred Irish draught mare, Carrie, in competitions for show jumping, long distance riding, and cross-country jumping. She also helped local riding schools with trail rides and remedial horses. Her interest in remedial horses led to a meeting with Monty Roberts when he gave a demonstration in Warwickshire. Roberts is well-known for his work with horses who have developed bad habits and for using "gentle" methods to get horses to work with humans. Twinney took a year's sabbatical from the constabulary to take Roberts' introductory course and eventually resigned from the police.

For the last five years Twinney has been living her dream as head instructor at the Monty Roberts International Learning Center in California. She is qualified as one of only eighteen Monty Roberts instructors in the world. The actual content of her work is quite broad and according to Twinney, includes "head instructor, examiner, course designer, horse trainer, and gentler." On the job she supervises instructors worldwide; designs, develops, and schedules courses for the center; teaches clinics and introductory and instructor courses; grades introductory and instructor students; and monitors and serves as a liaison for students. Her administrative functions include overseeing the office and equipment, promotion and publicity work, quality control, center board membership, and designing and developing team-building and leadership exercises. She also organizes farm tours and selects and oversees the students and interns.

Twinney also cares for a certain number of horses, administering medication when prescribed, starting and training young horses, maintaining any prescribed rehabilitation programs, and dealing with behavioral problems of remedial horses. She exercises and trains horses under saddle and handles young or untouched horses, including mustangs. Twinney's work also requires her to provide commentary for demonstrations for private organizations.

This entails great responsibility, but Twinney wouldn't have it any other way. She says, "I love the scope of learning, the chance to express oneself and help both humans and horses. I love the diversity and the unpredictability of the day's events." The only negative she can think of in her work does not really hinder her enjoyment of her job: "I understand the need for administration, but dislike the amount of paperwork," she admits.

The time she actually spends with horses varies, Twinney says, and depends upon the time of the year. For example, planning for the upcoming year does not involve working with horses. On the other hand, because she demonstrates the Monty Roberts method, she gets to "handle numerous horses in completely different circumstances on a daily basis."

Some of the specific skills that Twinney must know include Roberts' methods and concepts, especially the "round pen" and "join-up." Other facets of Roberts' training include "applications of human-horse methodology," which teaches parallels between horse and human psychology, what the horse is trying to teach humans, and how violence relates to the horse-human relationship. She must also have basic knowledge in stud management—including managing brood-mares and foals, handling studs, "foal imprinting, handling weanlings, and gentling stock"—horse anatomy and physiology, feeding and nutrition, conformation, and psychology. It is important for her to understand how the environment affects horses, the mental and physical aspects of horse development, and sport and holistic therapies. The remedial problems Twinney deals with include a horse's refusal to be caught or loaded onto a van or trailer; repetitive motions that arise from confinement ("stable vices"); and other behaviors, such as nipping, bucking, rearing, biting, kicking, and pulling back.

People in this type of job need to be approachable, empathetic, honest, fair, non-judgmental, open-minded, patient, calm, and flexible. "Being outgoing helps," Twinney adds. She must be punctual and professional, able to make decisions, handle pressure, and speak in public, especially to project her voice. Intelligence and the ability to "read people and horses" are also necessary.

Her advice to those interested in this type of career is to "follow your dreams and your heart. It's a bumpy road, but the experiences along the way are worth their weight in gold." For a job such as hers at the center, Twinney says that the ideal preparation is "Monty Roberts' own certification program." (Details are available on the website montyroberts.com.) Twinney also learns from other clinicians, including clinics or demonstrations run by Richard Shrake and Carolyn Resnick on natural horsemanship, Cindy Rackley on animal communication, and Dr. R. Miller on imprint training. She has a British diploma in Equine Herbal Natural Remedies and Aromatherapy, and she has studied reiki, "the Japanese art of hands-on healing." A common path for instructors is to "apply and work yourself up the ladder." Or, individuals qualified to instruct "can create a learning center most places in the world—there is room for all of us in different disciplines and aspects of the horse world."

Twinney sums up her feelings about her career and lifestyle this way: "There really aren't any typical days, and this is what makes it a wonderful career and way of life." In the future, she declares, "I want to make a difference in the horse world. I would love to help the American wild horse and take natural horsemanship to another level, especially to those in Third World countries." She describes horses as "strong and powerful" and has a deep faith in the joy and healing they can bring to the lives of others: "I believe that bringing this knowledge out into the open will benefit so many."

Profile
EQUESTRIENNE
Jill Henselwood

"My affinity for horses led me into show jumping," says Jill Henselwood, one of the premier international show jumpers in the world. "I enjoy the rewards of working with horses. They have full trust in me and give an incredible amount of themselves as we work together for a common goal."

Henselwood co-owns and operates Juniper Farms in Oxford Mills, Ontario, where she and her partner, Bob Henselwood, run a show jumping facility, coaching and training aspiring young grand prix riders and horses. Competing at the highest level of show jumping, Henselwood travels to competitions across the United States, Canada, and Europe, and always finds time to teach at numerous clinics nationwide.

Little wonder that, when asked to define her work, Henselwood produces a long list. "I teach, coach teams of international young riders, train horses, compete, buy and sell horses, manage equine and human competitive careers, and run a competitive show stable with all the business and financial arrangements that go along with that." But that's not all. "I also transport horses and work with the veterinary science field to help maintain and even increase the longevity of equine careers. And I have a working knowledge of blacksmithing!"

Henselwood probably did not know that work with horses would become her life when she first began riding at a summer camp at age five. Her talent for riding was obvious, however, and she began giving lessons to others when she was only ten. This led her to "catch riding" as a teenager. Catch riders show horses for other people, and while they may not always be paid, they gain a great deal of experience riding many different horses and working with many different people. To this role she brought her ability, enthusiasm, and helpful and friendly personality, producing wins for the horses and becoming friends with their owners.

She later apprenticed with international show jumper and coach Ian Millar for ten years, creating her own business at the same time. Under Millar's tutelage she gained an understanding of the business and the dedication and work ethic required to compete at the international level.

Henselwood made the Canadian Equestrian Team in 1991 and won her first international grand prix in 1992. From there she represented Canada at the World Cup Finals, World Championships, and Pan American games. She also qualified for the Canadian Olympic Team in 1996 and was ranked number one in Canada in 2001. ("Individual rankings change according to each year's results," she explains. "The results vary depending on the horses you have at the time and their experience at the top level.") In 2003 Henselwood competed in Europe, honing her skills at the premier competitions that are held every week. After being named Leading Grand Prix Rider on the 2004 Indio Desert Circuit, in California, Henselwood relocated her entire operation to Spruce Meadows in Calgary, the top jumping venue in the world.

Although the number of students and horses that she works with varies, Henselwood says that the "magic number" of students is ten. She usually has twenty to twenty-five horses in training and says that she can't really effectively manage more than that at one time. A typical day finds her training horses and coaching for the entire day.

In her training work with horses, Henselwood also relies upon her understanding of "the physiology of the horse." This helps her to set up the individual training and fitness programs for each animal. During the training programs, she rehearses technical exercises that simulate problems that each horse may encounter during competition. These programs are extremely important and must ensure that the horses peak at competition time and that they arrive keen, fit, well prepared, and confident.

Other work includes the administrative paperwork of the farm—billing, making entries, and keeping records. She juggles so many different things at one time that, she says, her mother often wonders how she keeps everything straight. She simply answers, "I am doing what I love."

Henselwood has a university degree in human kinetics with a minor in pedagogy (the study of teaching), and recommends a career path that supplements apprenticeships or other hands-on experience with a college education. She credits her education with "providing knowledge in many of the categories of my work." Where her coursework has not been as helpful, she realizes now, is in the business aspects of her work—"in looking after the tax incentives and investment opportunities available when acquiring grand prix horses."

Henselwood says that essential personal qualities for people who are interested in a career such as hers are "patience, enthusiasm, optimism, excess energy, discipline, and ambition." Enthusiasm and energy are especially important, she says, because the workdays are usually very long. Skills in communication and teaching are necessary for coaching. Natural riding ability, which is developed with years of experience, training, and competition, is vital, too.

Working closely with numerous people in many different roles—including owners, riders, and staff—makes having the ability to get along well with other people essential in her work. Another important, and less tangible, factor in her success is her personality. In addition to her work roles, she also has to interact extensively with the press and the general public. As she says, "Along the way it was my talent and my personality that helped me get many opportunities."

Henselwood enjoys the travel and the "hype of competition" her work provides. She also likes "participating in the development of an elite equine athlete and of talented young human athletes." What she doesn't like, she admits, is the "generally inconsistent levels of teaching in the sport."

Henselwood is quite positive about the way new technology has changed her work. "Technology has made it possible to do all facets of business right at the competition site," she says. "With today's technology we can have a portable office, and thus be more efficient during all of our business dealings."

Henselwood reminds prospective equestrians that "only the top two percent of athletes in any given sport can make a living by competing solely at their chosen sport. The rest need to earn money from their business knowledge, teaching, coaching, and so forth." While she has no regrets about the career choices she has made, she says, thoughtfully, "Incredible sacrifices must be made to get the opportunity to excel at this sport, and even more to seize them."

Chapter 4

Birds

I hope you love birds too. It is economical. It saves going to heaven.

Emily Dickinson

The widespread interest in birds is apparent from the numbers of bird feeders scattered throughout cities and suburbs and the many people who feed waterfowl at lakes and recreation areas. Another indication of the level of interest comes through a quick search of the Internet: websites about birds, birdwatching, bird feeding, bird species, and anything else about birds are legion. Many people who are interested in birds are simply lifelong hobbyists who join local clubs, actively watch the local bird life, and take the occasional birdwatching tour. Others pour their enthusiasm into their work and find jobs that deal with birds.

Ornithology is the study of birds. This broad field includes many different niches that cover practically every aspect of bird life. Jobs in ornithology run the gamut from highly specialized scientists—a great many of whom work in conservation biology and as academics—to field ornithologists, bird trainers, naturalists, educators, bird tour leaders, artists, and preservationists. Ornithologists can study bird populations, avian physiology, or how birds evolved.

Others study birds and changes relative to today's environment and the effect of future ecological changes on birds. In March 2004, BirdLife International issued a report known as the State of the World's Birds. This report is the first time all the current research about birds has been brought together into one document, and it does not offer good news for birds or bird lovers. For one thing, the report notes that out of a total of almost 9,000 bird species, 1,211 are threatened by factors such as climate change, deforestation of many tropical habitats, and invasive species that have vastly changed the ecosystems of ocean islands. Birds are good indicators of overall environmental health, which makes these threats especially troubling.

The study of birds is an area where non-professionals can make significant contributions. Volunteers often participate in the annual bird counts that take place around the world. Because the interest in birds and birdwatching—often known as birding—is increasing, work for the leaders of birdwatching tours is also on the rise. Some organizations plan tours for birders to areas of the world where unique and exotic birds can be found.

Aviculture relates to the care, housing, and feeding of birds in captivity. Aviculturists work in zoos or bird parks, taking care of all aspects of the lives of these birds, including feeding them, monitoring their health, and cleaning the exhibits. Bird curators manage the overall daily operations of a bird department as well as the long-range planning. They are responsible for the health of the birds in the collection and work on the breeding program, if their institution has one.

Most bird training serves to make a bird's institutional care easier and their display more interesting and educational for visitors, although animal trainers have also trained birds for roles in movies. The owls in the Harry Potter movies, for example, had to be trained to fly through open windows and pick up and carry objects—not normal bird behaviors. According to an October 2002 Reuters news item, animal trainer Gary Gero considered successfully training the owls for these movies one of his most difficult tasks; training birds to perform these tasks had never been done before that time.

This chapter lists a number of jobs that deal with birds. Additional work with birds is done by wildlife rehabilitators (for more information, see Chapter 7) and poultry farmers (see Chapter 8). Keep in mind that the job title is less important than the content of the work. Different institutions and businesses structure and name jobs differently, and some may use one of these titles for a position that requires all or most of the types of work described on the following pages.

AVICULTURE

Salary Range: Curators earn between $30,000 and $65,000. Other aviculture positions earn between $19,000 and $30,000.

Educational Requirements: Most aviculture positions require a bachelor's or associate's degree in biological sciences.

Employment Outlook: Dependent upon zoo expansion; jobs currently appear to be static.

The general responsibilities of aviculture workers include feeding birds, cleaning exhibits, and monitoring the health of all birds kept in a specific institution. A few positions with somewhat different responsibilities fall under the general heading of aviculture, several of which are described in this section.

Bird Curator

The bird curator manages the aviculture department and oversees daily operations. He or she monitors the health and the dietary habits of the birds, ensuring that they are fed an appropriate diet and developing new diets as required. Curators are in charge of breeding programs, which may entail working with curators in locations around the world to promote species survival. They also help in developing new animal exhibits.

A bird curator's work may require long hours, and it can also involve travel—sometimes on very short notice and for long periods of time—to transfer animals to different parks, consult with other curators, or attend zoological meetings. The job often involves a fair amount of physical work, mostly lifting and carrying heavy loads. People with experience working with birds—for example, those who have volunteered in different institutions or helped with rehabilitation—will have gained many useful skills for curatorial work and will have an edge in getting a job.

Aviculture Supervisor

Aviculture supervisors (sometimes known as bird department supervisors) have overall administrative responsibility for the aviculture department of a zoo or animal park. These individuals do little direct work with birds; their function is to oversee the daily operations of the department. Hiring, training, and scheduling of staff are their primary duties. They maintain all records, oversee animal transportation, and are sometimes involved in education programs. They must also see that all aviculture exhibits are properly maintained so that the birds are healthy, and may work with other animal departments. Aviculture supervisors must have good management skills to ensure that the animals receive the appropriate care.

Aviculturist

Aviculturists (sometimes known as bird keepers) have the most hands-on contact with birds. They prepare and distribute food to the birds in the collection, clean and maintain the bird exhibits, keep records that include the type and amount of food at each feeding, and spend time observing the behavior of the birds and watching for possible health problems.

Because the work can be physically taxing, aviculturists need to be in good shape. The work often puts aviculturists in contact with unpleasant odors. At times the work may require twenty-four-hour care of newly hatched birds or of birds that have been critically injured.

BIRD TOUR LEADER

Salary Range: Extremely varied.

Educational Requirements: Academic background in biological sciences beneficial; main requirement is an in-depth knowledge of birds and the ability to find and identify them quickly.

Employment Outlook: Good, as interest in birding continues to increase.

As the popularity of birding has increased, so has the number of bird tours available to the intrepid birder. Bird tour agencies often conduct tours to sites all over the world where interesting and unique birds can be found. Bird tour leaders do the hands-on work during these tours. They must be able to interact well with all kinds of people and help them to see birds, especially individuals with little birding experience. Thus, general people skills are essential. Tour leaders need to have vast knowledge about birds, especially the birds of the area covered by the tour, as well as the areas to which these tours travel.

They must be very good at identifying different birds, both by sight and sound. Because many persons who sign up for tours already have a high degree of skill in bird identification, the tour leader must be an indisputable and acknowledged identification authority.

Because their workday often includes preparation and planning, tour leaders may work long and tiring hours: twenty-hour days are not uncommon. They must be able to handle all possible in-the-field situations and emergencies. Considering the variety of tasks tour leaders must accomplish, time management skills are essential.

FIELD ORNITHOLOGIST

Salary Range: Usually between $30,000 to $55,000, but varies tremendously.

Educational Requirements: Minimum requirement for most positions is a bachelor of science in zoology; many jobs require a master's degree or a Ph.D. Experience helps in gaining positions.

Employment Outlook: The number of jobs is not increasing. The field is very competitive.

Field ornithologists are employed by conservation organizations, universities, the U.S. Forest Service, state governments, regional governments, private companies, wildlife refuges, and national forests and parks. As the name implies, most of them work in the outdoors. They monitor bird populations, conducting regular surveys in specific areas and tracking a population's numbers over a period of time. They also monitor bird health in a given area and often collect dead birds in the process.

Bird identification skills are essential in this work. Species must be identified by sight—whether in flight, on the ground, in a tree, or in the water—and by sound. Field ornithologists must be able to differentiate birds by gender and variations in plumage. Different geographical locations may require a specialized knowledge of bird types—shorebirds in a coastal area or songbirds in an interior location, for example.

In addition to having excellent observation skills, field ornithologists must have patience and be accurate in recording their observations. They must be able to enter information on the computer and use a variety of highly technical computer programs, such as geographic information systems that help in analyzing landscape data. Good verbal and written communication skills are essential, as many positions involve writing reports and communicating with the general public. Field ornithologists also need to work well with others. Often research work is done by two or more individuals working together to cover a specific area, and team members must be able to live and work together in close quarters and in isolated settings for extended periods of time. Supervisory skills are important for higher-level positions.

Because field ornithology requires travel, a valid driver's license is essential. The hours can be long and often include weekend work. Additionally, field conditions vary tremendously from hot to cold and often include remote locations and rugged terrain. Field ornithologists must be able to tolerate challenging environmental conditions. The work is physically strenuous and is often conducted at night or in the very early morning.

The ability to research ecological or restoration issues as they apply to conservation, management, or habitat restoration is an important part of field ornithologist's work. They may need to study habitat use, reproduction of birds in an area, effects of landscape changes on the avian population, patterns of migration, and other issues that deal with ecology and conservation. They may also be required to be knowledgeable about plant species and able to identify them in the area where they are working. Some positions require the ability to suggest strategies to preserve plant life in the location where bird species are being studied.

BIRD TRAINER

Salary Range: Varies, but generally is in the range of $15,000 to $35,000.

Educational Requirements: Four-year life sciences degree for work in zoos; some two-year degrees are available.

Employment Outlook: Job demand is currently limited but expected to increase.

Most bird trainers work in zoos, nature centers, and private facilities that have bird collections. A rare few work with movies and television programs. Some trainers have a specialty in training birds but may also train other animal species.

The types of behaviors that bird trainers teach vary. They usually include natural behaviors so that visitors can learn about birds and conservation. This is often the case in outreach programs of zoos, nature centers, private facilities, or special programs that educate the public about vanishing species. These programs may travel to various locations, or they may be presentations located at a specific facility. Trainers may also work as part of a team to design a new habitat or education program for a zoo.

Other behaviors that bird trainers work to teach birds are those that contribute to their health and welfare; these are known as husbandry behaviors. Examples include standing on a scale and moving voluntarily from one enclosure to another. These behaviors eliminate some of the stresses birds experience in captivity.

Falconry, a specialized type of bird training in which raptors are taught to hunt prey on command, is mostly a hobby. However, some falconers do make a living by training birds of prey to serve as deterrents to "nuisance birds," such as seagulls and geese, that plague airports, golf courses, and dumps. (The danger of birds at airports is well documented—big flying birds can threaten the safety of aircraft.) This activity is known as abatement.

Bird training is also important for the process of releasing captive-born birds into the wild. Bird trainers were used extensively, for example, in the recent, highly publicized California condor reintroduction program to prepare the birds for survival in the wild.

Other trainers work with birds kept as pets, including, most commonly, parrots. Pet parrots may develop problem behaviors, such as biting or screaming, that are quite annoying to owners. Bird trainers can help owners learn the causes of the problems and how to control them.

An essential quality for good bird trainers is patience. They must also be sensitive to the behaviors of the birds, understand the ways in which human actions affect bird behavior, and have a solid working knowledge of conditioning theories. Trainers need to be able to work long, hard days in sometimes dirty conditions; they must also clean cages, scrub water bowls, and attend to their birds' health care needs.

Bird trainers must also enjoy working with people and educating others. Often bird trainers instruct other trainers in zoos or elsewhere in the use of conditioning methods.

A bachelor's degree in the life sciences is important background for this work. Experience, however, is also invaluable and can be obtained through volunteer work, internships (which are either low-paying or simply well-supervised volunteer work) and part-time work. Bird trainers often start work in an institution at a low-level position and then work up to their desired job.

Bird trainers typically spend a lot of time outdoors, caring for birds in all kinds of weather. The work can involve heavy lifting and running and be very physically demanding. It may involve making or repairing cages, installing perches, and climbing ladders.

See profile on page 88.
Additional trainer information on pages 12, 64, and 101.

RESOURCES

American Bird Conservancy
P.O. Box 249
The Plains, VA 20198
phone: 540-253-5780
fax: 540-253-5782
email: abc@abcbirds.org
www.abcbirds.org

American Birding Association
P.O. Box 6599
Colorado Springs, CO 80934-6599
phone: 800-850-2473
fax: 719-578-1480
email: member@aba.org
www.americanbirding.org

American Federation of Aviculture
P.O. Box 7312
North Kansas City, MO 64116
phone: 816-421-2473
fax: 816-421-3214
email: afaoffice@aol.com
www.afabirds.org

American Ornithologists' Union (AOU)
Suite 402
1313 Dolley Madison Boulevard
McLean, VA 22101
email: aou@burkinc.com
www.aou.org

Association of Field Ornithologists (AFO)
c/o Allen Press
P.O. Box 1897
Lawrence, KS 66044-1897
www.afonet.org

Avicultural Advancement Council of Canada
P.O. Box 123
Chemainus, British Columbia
Canada V0R 1K0
phone: 250-246-4803
fax: 250-246-4912
email: exec@aacc.ca
www.aacc.ca

International Association of Avian Trainers and Educators
350 St. Andrews Fairway
Memphis, TN 38111
phone: 901-685-9122
fax: 901-685-7233
email: secretary@iaate.org
www.iaate.org

National Audubon Society
700 Broadway
New York, NY 10003
phone: 212-979-3000
fax: 212-979-3188
www.audubon.org
(Also has state and county chapters)

Ornithological Societies of North America (OSNA)
P.O. Box 1897
Lawrence, KS 66044
phone: 800-627-0629
fax: 785-843-1274
email: osna@allenpress.com
www.nmnh.si.edu

Profile

BIRD TRAINER
Barb Heidenreich

"On my job I am constantly challenged to learn more," says bird trainer Barb Heidenreich enthusiastically. "There are close to nine thousand bird species identified in the world. I learn something new every day."

Working out of Austin, Texas, she both trains birds as well as some other animal species and bird trainers. She owns two businesses. As the owner of Animal Training and Consulting Services, she has consulted in facilities around the world, including the Dallas World Aquarium, the John Ball Zoo in Michigan, the Caldwell Zoo in Texas, and the African Safari in Mexico. She has also worked with several Disney facilities, the Chicago Zoological Society, the Perth Zoo in Australia, Ocean Park in Hong Kong, and the Umgeni River Bird Park in South Africa. Her job at these facilities has been to teach training techniques and help develop bird shows.

As part of this business, Heidenreich also assists her clients in evaluating current staff and acquiring new staff and birds for a specific show. She trains the staff and birds, ensures that bird housing is suitable, produces the show, and works on other aspects that go into making the event a success. She also evaluates current programs at facilities that are experiencing problems and works to solve these problems and increase the programs' entertainment value. (When Heidenreich talks about entertainment, she doesn't mean something that is disrespectful to the animals—she means programs that get watchers interested and excited about learning about birds and various aspects of their life.)

As the owner of Good Bird Consulting, her second business, Heidenreich works with parrots that have developed peculiar behaviors and helps their owners understand the cause of the behaviors and how to change them.

Ever since her childhood, Heidenreich has loved animals. In addition to enjoying household pets, she searched for wildlife in the suburbs where she grew up. She volunteered to assist a local veterinarian during her high school years, and her courses in both high school and college focused on the life sciences. During college she obtained a great variety of work-study positions that involved animals, assisting in studies on song sparrow dialect, lizard territorial behavior, equine care, wildlife rehabilitation, and salamander genetics.

By the time she had obtained her degree in zoology, Heidenreich had decided that she wanted to be a zookeeper. To get her foot in the door, she accepted a low-paying position in the education department of a nearby zoo. Her role there—caring for the animals that were involved in the outreach education program—gave her her first exposure to animal training. She had to ensure that the animals in the program were comfortable with traveling and being around large groups of children.

"I really felt I had discovered what I enjoyed most about working with animals," she remembers. "I loved having the opportunity to develop a relationship with an animal that was based on positive interactions. I was hooked on training." When a position opened up in the zoo's bird show department, Heidenreich snapped it up and began training birds full time. That was in 1990, and she has never looked back. Since those early days, she has literally been around the world in the course of doing her work.

Heidenreich spends a lot of time working outdoors. The daily care of animals, whatever the weather conditions, is an essential part of her work. Her responsibilities can be quite physically demanding and sometimes include heavy lifting. She often builds or modifies bird cages for her charges. She works directly with the birds when training them. And if she is training other trainers, she interacts directly with them as well, observing their methods and teaching them new approaches. When consulting, she works closely with facility workers to organize and develop strategies to meet their goals. After these strategies have been developed, she usually spends the whole day "working with the staff and birds in a facility."

The tremendous variation in her work and work locations make describing a typical day difficult. "A typical day may involve checking the health of all the animals, weighing birds, cleaning cages, and preparing diets," says Heidenreich. "After the basics are done, we begin training the birds for the day. I do some of the training and handling, but mostly I am there to help the staff members of the facility learn how to apply training concepts. When we are setting up a program, we spend a lot of time training each day. By the end of the day we usually just need to make sure everyone is settled in for the night and write up our training reports." Because she owns and operates two businesses, she must also spend time developing these businesses, networking and writing proposals for contracts.

On the days that she is training the animals, however, Heidenreich says that she spends about three-quarters of the day directly with the animals. In addition to the actual training, this time is spent cleaning cages and water bowls, "developing presentations, providing enrichment, administering to health care needs, and feeding." A lot of this interaction is very hands-on. Compared to other animal careers, "I think animal training gives an individual many opportunities to work very closely with animals."

Personality traits that Heidenreich emphasizes as important for her career are being both an "animal person" and a "people person." She says: "In my situation, we are training animals to educate the public about conservation. That means we need to be able to talk to people as well."

She also emphasizes the importance of being able "to improvise and think on your feet. Birds don't always do exactly what you expect during a presentation. It is helpful to be able to talk to an audience while you figure out what you are going to do about the bird that is sitting in the tree ignoring you during the show." Another important quality is creativity, because there are many different ways to get birds to adopt a specific behavior.

Heidenreich enjoys almost all aspects of her work. She finds the science of behavior fascinating, and enjoys meeting and teaching people from all over the world. "I also cherish the opportunities I have had to work with so many interesting animals. They are just amazing," she says enthusiastically. When pressed to mention a downside to her work, she does admit that "the most challenging part of the job is spending a lot of time on the road."

Typical paths to training birds and other animals, are, says Heidenreich, usually through veterinary-type positions or work at pet stores. Others may take the route she took—beginning in a lower-level zookeeper position and working up to a training job. "In any case," Heidenreich says, "I do think the combination of hands-on experience and education are essential to success in the animal training field." The education that she recommends is a bachelor's of science degree in the life sciences with complementary experience from volunteer and part-time work.

Heidenreich is very positive about the role of technology in training work. "New record-keeping systems have been developed that make keeping records much easier," she says. "It is possible to communicate with trainers all over the world quite easily. Interesting innovations have been created to facilitate exciting and educational conservation presentations."

Her advice to someone who wants to pursue a career in animal training is to learn as much as possible about conditioning and how it works. "Spend as much time as you can around animals. Try to learn how to read and interpret animal behavior. Notice how what you do can affect animal behavior. Learn to be sensitive so that you do not cause an animal to be fearful or aggressive."

Although Heidenreich does not recommend bird training as a way to get rich quickly—she points out that pay in zoos and nature centers is notoriously low—she has found the work to be deeply satisfying. And she sees the field of animal training as a growing one. "More people have an interest in how to train animals using positive reinforcement."

When it comes to getting a job in this field, Heidenreich emphasizes the value of networking and getting your foot in the door at a facility that you like. "You may have to take a job that is not your ideal," she says, "or you may have to volunteer first before you get the job that allows you to train an animal."

Chapter 5

Marine Animals, Fish, and Other Aquatic Creatures

If you were to make little fishes talk, they would talk like whales.

Oliver Goldsmith

When dealing with creatures that live in the water, it is common to divide them into two different types. Aquatic animals live in a freshwater environment, while marine animals live in a saltwater environment. The ocean is the largest marine environment on earth; the smaller environments of lakes, rivers, streams, and wetlands are mainly freshwater. The creatures that inhabit aquatic and marine environments are many and varied.

This chapter covers work with these animals, including marine mammals as well as smaller species such as fish or algae, which are used for food and educational purposes. It looks at work with these animals in their natural environment as well as in aquariums and other man-made settings.

Jobs involving water animals include researcher, field biologist, laboratory worker, animal trainer, veterinarian, whalewatching guide, naturalist, and educator. Government and private agencies also employ people who work on legislation, management, conservation, and welfare issues. Other positions involving water animals include curating museum displays and collections and working as an artist, photographer, or filmmaker. The work of individuals such as Jacques Cousteau and Sylvia Earle, as shown in movies and on TV, may make work with aquatic animals seem glamorous and attractive. In reality, most of these jobs are not always as exciting as they appear. The work can involve long days at sea, working under a relentless sun, or spending hours in the laboratory or on computers. It may also involve hauling heavy buckets of fish for the animals, cleaning a dirty body of water, writing reports and grant applications, and applying for permits. Nevertheless, to many people, work with marine and aquatic animals is extremely satisfying.

The best preparation for work with water creatures is a background in the basic sciences—biology, chemistry, and physics—and mathematics and computers. Because the field is so highly competitive, a specialized scientific skill (such as acoustics, genetics, biomolecular analysis, or biostatistics), a dual major in school, or extensive experience may provide an edge in getting a good job.

Employers in this field include international, federal, state, and local government agencies. Some of the prominent U.S. federal agencies are the National Oceanic and Atmospheric Administration, National Marine Fisheries Service, the Fish and Wildlife Service, the Biological Resources Discipline of the U.S. Geological Survey, the Office of Naval Research, the Marine Mammal Commission, the National Park Service, the National Science Foundation, and the Smithsonian Institution. Rescue centers for marine mammals, such as the Marine Mammal Center in California, also provide some work. Canadian federal government offices include Agriculture Canada, Canadian Wildlife Service, and Fisheries and Oceans Canada. Provincial departments vary, depending upon the location of the province. Agriculture and Fisheries or Ministry of Natural Resources is the first place to check for employers.

Industries whose work in the ocean may affect marine mammals, such as oil and gas exploration and sea transportation, often hire marine biologists, as do commercial fishing operations. Other positions can be found with environmental, advocacy, and animal welfare organizations. Oceanariums (sea water aquariums), aquariums, and zoos hire marine biologists and other positions. Some jobs are also available in museums in the areas of educational programs, research, and curatorial positions.

Note: In this chapter the term "marine biologist" is used as a general name for any work involving the study of marine animal behavior.

AQUACULTURE/FISH HATCHERIES

Salary Range: Starting salaries are about $16,000 to $24,000; with experience, they can reach or exceed the upper $30,000 range.

Educational Requirements: Entry-level positions require a high school diploma; more education will lead to better positions. Higher-level positions require a bachelor of science degree or an advanced degree with an emphasis in aquaculture.

Employment Outlook: Good. Fisheries and hatcheries are one of the fastest-growing sectors of the agricultural industry.

Aquaculture is the process of using artificial techniques to cultivate and produce aquatic plants and animals, such as fish, shrimp, clams, kelp, and algae. Aquaculture is often described as agriculture for the oceans, because it involves growing and harvesting aquatic life for human consumption. The rapid expansion of this field is illustrated by studies that indicate that more than fifteen percent of the fish and seafood consumed worldwide is now produced by aquaculture. With the expected increase in the demand for fish, the need for aquaculture is also expected to increase.

The basic duties in aquaculture are maintaining the physical units, following the feeding schedule, and treating diseases. Occasionally the fish or aquatic wildlife will need to be transported or stocked in lakes and rivers. Additional work can include building or repairing equipment, giving tours of the aquaculture facility, and assisting the biological or research staff on field projects.

Aquaculture is a relatively new field and few university programs offer degrees in it, although some do offer aquaculture courses or have an emphasis in aquaculture. People going into this field should take courses in biology, technology, management, and marketing.

Fish hatcheries are often operated by governmental agencies, and the fish grown there are used to stock or restock streams, rivers, and lakes. Work in hatcheries goes on at three levels. Fish management technicians work directly in the production and care of the fish, much the same as the basic jobs in aquaculture. Fish hatchery coordinators supervise the work of the technicians and the overall work of the hatchery; individuals in this position also monitor the environment into which the fish will be released, oversee the transportation and stocking activities, and prepare monthly and annual reports. Fish management supervisors oversee the operation of all fish hatcheries and fish hatchery workers.

Government aquaculture jobs can involve management of natural resources as well as work at facilities where fish are raised to stock public waters, different species are grown for recovery programs, and genetic research is conducted. Other government workers consult with hatchery managers.

In industry, commercial aquaculture is growing rapidly and provides many jobs. The main goal here, however, is to grow aquatic animals to be used for human consumption. Positions in commercial aquaculture range from various managers, including business managers, to the technicians. Some positions in aquaculture are for professors at universities. The hands-on work in the actual hatchery facility is, however, done by technicians. In the future, as this field continues to grow, more aquaculture jobs should open up in education; these may place greater emphasis on researching and teaching new technologies and practices for this field.

AQUARIST

Salary Range: Varies greatly, depending on institution and individual experience and background. The average starting salary is from $17,200 to $25,800 a year; the median is around $26,000 to $30,000 but can go to $45,000.

Educational Requirements: Minimum of a bachelor's of science in biology or related field.

Employment Outlook: Promising, when there are new aquariums and aquarium expansion; the field is very competitive, however.

Strictly speaking, an aquarist is someone who maintains an aquarium. An aquarist is also a curator, the person in charge of the collection of animals in an aquarium. Aquarists may also find work in studying aquatic life.

Aquarists are responsible for the day-to-day care of marine and freshwater animals in an aquarium setting. They also maintain the physical environment of these animals and may be involved in collecting marine animals or plants necessary for display. The job involves much physical work, such as scrubbing and cleaning the aquarium to keep it clean. The work can also be very dirty—cleaning galleys, preparing fish, and so forth—and very demanding. It is rarely a nine-to-five job—because the work is with animals who depend upon the aquarist, a problem can't be put off for another day, but must be taken care of immediately.

Caring for aquarium animals includes preparing food to the specifications for that particular species and feeding it to the animals. Observing animal behavior and health is another component of an aquarist's duties: he or she is responsible for recognizing when an animal is behaving in an unusual fashion or looks unhealthy. Aquarists also administer prescribed medical treatments for sick or diseased animals.

Aquarists must understand water chemistry and be able to maintain the water quality needed for the biological processes in aquarium habitats. Aquarium filtration, known as life support, is a very technical system which aquarists must be expert in understanding and monitoring. They must be able to build or repair these systems as necessary. Aquarists need to be able to work well as part of a team yet also be self-motivated and able to work well on their own. Because aquarists work in water so much of the time, scuba certification is essential. Aquarists must be able to research the essentials of feeding and caring for the animals.

Volunteering and unpaid, or very low-paying, internships are essential steps in the process of obtaining a full-time position as an aquarist. When full-time jobs are available, an individual who has already worked in that aquarium as a volunteer or intern has a distinct advantage in getting a job, as the organization already knows that person's work. Knowledge of, or a specialty in, a specific type of marine environment can also be an advantage.

See profile on page 109.

FISHERIES MANAGEMENT

Salary Range: Average entry-level salary is around $27,170; mid-level is about $33,693; senior level is around $55,000 to $65,000. Salaries differ from setting to setting.

Educational Requirements: Entry-level technicians need a bachelor's degree in fisheries biology, wildlife management, aquatic biology, or a related field. Biologist positions need a master's degree and work experience in fisheries management or research.

Employment Outlook: Good; the number of jobs in this area is expected to increase as conservation concerns become more important.

Fisheries management is at its core the process of managing populations of fish and their environments so that others can enjoy fishing. Fisheries management can be especially rewarding work for individuals who like to fish. Workers in this field choose from several different types of jobs: research biologist, management biologist, or fisheries biologist.

Research biologists study the size of fish populations, how fish relate to other aquatic life, how contaminants affect aquatic life, and how different species are distributed. They study the habitat requirements of aquatic life, fish behaviors, and the kinds and prevalence of disease among aquatic animals. They also study management practices that will improve natural fisheries. Often, if a waterway is quite large and takes in a number of different states or countries, these responsibilities demand cooperation with staff from the other regions. (See the research biologist entry on page 103.)

Management biologists use the information developed by research biologists in the field to design ways to improve fish populations and fishing opportunities for anglers. They are tasked with stocking bodies of water with fish, controlling water levels and vegetation, and working to improve water quality to help natural spawning. They are also involved with developing and implementing fishing regulations, improving fish habitats, and conducting environmental assessments. By constructing and maintaining shoreline fishing areas or boat ramps they provide essential services to anglers; one of their ongoing concerns is making fishing facilities available to individuals with mobility disadvantages. Publicizing information on fisheries is another part of the work of management biologists. This involves work on publications and with clinics and education programs. Public speaking is an important part of a management biologist's job. He or she is often called upon to speak on topics that range from stewardship of aquatic resources to responsible angling.

Fisheries biologists monitor and evaluate species or populations by taking samples; they also evaluate habitats, implementing enhancement projects where necessary. They work with the public by offering educational programs, providing technical assistance to public and private landowners, and developing aquatic community management plans and fishing regulations. Fisheries biologists also conduct environmental assessments and evaluate fish kills looking for causes and contributing factors. In the summertime they mainly work outside, in all kinds of weather. Their work may take them across an entire state, depending upon their employer. They need to be able to work well with others, as they will often be part of a team, as well as to be able to work independently. Major employers of fisheries biologists are city, country, state, and federal governments, though recently some progressive private corporations have begun to hire them.

MARINE COLLECTOR

Salary Range: Varies; typical water-based jobs begin around $24,000 with a twenty percent increase every five years.
Educational Requirements: Extensive experience in a marine environment; scuba certification essential.
Employment Outlook: The work is strongly connected to the economy, and falters in a weak economy.

Various animal and plant species are collected from the seas for a variety of reasons. In today's world of improved and efficient aquariums, it is now possible to establish aquariums in homes, classrooms, and research laboratories. This allows students to examine various species, provided they can be supplied, without needing to observe them in the wild or go to a large aquarium that may be some distance away.

Collected species are also needed for research. For example, shrimp are often used in studies of pollution. Collectors may be asked to supply shrimp to private or government organizations that are researching the effects of polluted water. Additionally, specimens are used to feed captive marine animals and are sold to home hobbyists.

(As home aquariums have increased in popularity, so has the need for different types of fish to sell to hobbyists.)

Collecting live specimens is, then, the principal job of marine collectors. To do this, they go out into the marine environment, where they are subject to the vagaries of wind, temperature, and tide. Sometimes finding the desired species in the quantity needed is relatively easy, but at other times it can be quite difficult. Collectors, therefore, need to understand and respect the environment in which they search for species.

In addition to collecting actual specimens of marine animals, collectors also bring in algae that have both functional—filtration, food, and water quality—and decorative uses in a marine aquarium. A collector needs to thoroughly understand the different types of algae, however; many varieties actually have a negative effect on aquarium environments.

The ability to do the actual collecting, while the most important part of the occupation, is not the only skill needed in this work. Because specimens need to arrive alive and in good condition, transportation and handling are almost as important as the initial collection. The transportation for each order must be planned carefully. Additionally, marine collectors need to know about the life support equipment used to keep the species they collect alive until they can be safely delivered to their destination.

Scuba and snorkeling skills are essential for marine collectors. They must be thoroughly knowledgeable in the use of this equipment as well as water and marine conditions conducive to collecting.

Marine collectors often work on a freelance basis or for organizations that supply aquariums. Other jobs can be found with various government branches and sometimes for universities that have extensive marine biology programs. Because many aquariums get significant funding from the admission-paying public, they suffer when the economy suffers. And when the economy undergoes a downturn, marine collectors who work for aquariums are among the first to feel the pinch.

See profile on page 112.

MARINE MAMMAL TRAINER

Salary Range: Varies by setting, but in general pay starts between $17,000 and $25,000 and averages around $35,000.

Educational Requirements: Most positions require a bachelor of science degree, scuba certification, and prior experience.

Employment Outlook: There are few aquariums around the world, competition for jobs is intense, and turnover is small.

Marine mammal trainers have a very interesting and very intense job. They work with and care for marine mammals, including dolphins, whales, seals, walruses, and sea lions. Their main responsibility, above all else, is to maintain and enhance the health and well-being of the animals that are in their care.

For many trainers, the actual training of the animals is the most pleasant and interesting part of their job. Trainers teach mammals to do new tricks for public shows and review the tricks they've already learned to ensure that they are not forgotten. Trainers also teach "husbandry behaviors" that are not seen by the public but allow trainers to check on the health of these creatures—for example, allowing trainers to take blood samples or examine their body parts.

Trainers need to spend time playing with the animals. Such sessions help to cement the bond between trainer and animal and provide pleasant experiences for both. Marine mammal trainers are also responsible for the mental health of the animals, and play can improve an animal's mental health.

A major job of the trainers is to feed the animals in their care. This task is difficult; marine mammals can consume between ten to two hundred pounds of fish a day. The trainer prepares the food and gives the animals the specially formulated vitamins essential to maintain their health.

Another very important task for a trainer is to monitor the health of the animals. Detailed daily record-keeping of the food consumed, the amount of time spent in training and play, and the shows in which they perform is vital in this respect. Trainers regularly record respiration rates and take blood samples, and a veterinarian visits all aquarium animals on a regular basis. These accurate and up-to-date records help trainers track changes in appetite and in behavior patterns.

Cleaning the animal habitat is also an important task. The habitat must be kept clean and the water kept at strict levels of pH, alkalinity, salinity, and temperature to keep the environment comfortable for the animal. Additionally, the food preparation area must be kept sanitary to avoid the spread of germs.

Trainers interact with the public through their role in presenting the animals doing tricks and leading interpretation sessions, which usually includes answering questions. Marine mammal trainers realize that educating the public is essential to help develop an understanding and respect for marine life that will ensure its survival.

Generally, marine mammal trainers spend about half of their time working with the animals and the other half doing the myriad of other necessary tasks: cleaning, preparing food, record-keeping, and working with the public.

Training is not strictly a nine-to-five job. At times a trainer may work around the clock, especially when caring for a sick animal. In many aquariums, trainers are required to be on call twenty-four hours a day, and they may be required to work every day of the week. Trainers frequently work outdoors, in all kinds of weather. On warm, sunny days, this can be quite pleasant. It is less so during cold and inclement weather. The job requires a strong commitment on the part of the trainer. Marine mammal trainers generally work as part of a team and they need strong teamwork skills and the ability to communicate well with other team members.

Essential qualities for any marine mammal trainer are compassion and a very strong love for animals. Some of these animals are quite large, so trainers also need to exercise care in dealing with them. Trainers need to be able to think clearly, make quick decisions, exercise common sense, maintain a calm and even disposition, and explain things to others. Patience is essential, because training animals can be frustrating and time-consuming. This is not a job for people who need immediate gratification or dislike repetition. Finally, of course, a love of water and aquatic environments is very important.

Although a bachelor's degree with courses in biology and zoology is a common requirement for this career, experience in working with animals is also crucial. People interested in this kind of work should begin volunteering with animals as soon as possible. Volunteer work has the added benefit of helping prospective trainers decide whether they have the dedication that will carry them through the often intensive and tiring workday. Individuals who have taken animal technician courses and have a great deal of experience working with animals may have a distinct edge in obtaining the few jobs available in marine mammal training. Succeeding in a job may be just as difficult as finding one, so every opportunity for gaining experience should be taken.

In the future, rehabilitation of injured marine mammals may become a more important part of work for marine mammal trainers. As well, the field is now in the process of changing its focus from entertainment to education.

Additional training information on pages 12, 64, 84, and 88.

RESEARCH BIOLOGIST (FISHERIES)

Salary Range: Depends upon level of work; varies from $25,000 to $53,000.

Educational Requirements: Minimum of a bachelor's degree with research experience; most positions need at least a master's degree, and many require a doctorate.

Employment Outlook: Depends partly on public interest in preserving and enhancing natural fisheries.

Jobs in this field, as in so many others, go under different titles, including fisheries research biologist, aquatic biologist, and aquatic ecologist. A research biologist can work in many areas not related to marine biology.

Research biologists study different types of fish or different fish habitats. The work may involve researching the behavior of animals in captivity, or it may deal with problems in conservation and management of different species of fish in the wild. Areas of study may include diet, reproduction, and population growth. Depending on the level of the position, a biologist will be responsible for initiating research or coordinating research with others. Often the work is with state departments of fisheries and wildlife, where the focus is on managing different species in the wild and, where necessary, working to restore a species to its natural habitat. In these cases, research biologists design and initiate studies to assess the population of a species and provide information on factors that have led to problems with the species. They work with teams to overcome these factors and provide continuing management input into restoration efforts. An additional part of this work is providing information to landowners to help them more effectively manage their land so that it benefits aquatic habitats in important watershed areas.

Research is done both in the field and the laboratory. Outside work may involve walking distances in rugged terrain and carrying heavy loads of equipment—research biologists need to be physically fit. Sometimes extensive laboratory work is needed, particularly if a problem appears to be microbial, not strictly environmental. Research biologists need skills in and evaluating research findings—they need to identify, quantify, summarize, and interpret the data that has been collected. They may also need to make decisions in the field. A driver's license is usually essential, as the work may involve travel over a large territory.

Research biologists must be able to work independently and work well with others, particularly within multidisciplinary teams, in reaching a consensus. They need to be able to swim well and operate boats and motors; they also need to be scuba-certified. During fieldwork, they may need to work long, irregular hours and on the weekends. Additionally, they have to be able to create computer databases and use statistical packages to analyze information.

Research biologists also need to possess top-notch research, writing, and communication skills. They often need to locate relevant data in the existing literature and prepare various reports and grant applications. They also need the ability to make presentations to a diverse audience that may consist of either peers or individuals with no knowledge of the subject area.

The greatest number of research biologist jobs can be found with state departments of fish and wildlife, in both coastal states as well as states with large numbers of lakes and rivers. The U.S. Forest Service also has some positions for fisheries biologists. Provincial departments of fisheries and Fisheries and Oceans Canada are places to look for work in Canada. Some jobs are also available with engineering firms that specialize in environmental issues relating to water policy, fish habitat, and regulatory matters. Jobs are also available with native tribes seeking to preserve their way of life and with large aquariums that conduct research in marine biology.

RESOURCES

American Fisheries Society
5410 Grosvenor Lane
Bethesda, MD 20814
phone: 301-897-8616
fax: 301-897-8096
email: main@fisheries.org
www.fisheries.org

American Institute of Biological Sciences (AIBS)
1444 I Street, NW, Suite 200
Washington, DC 20005
phone: 202-628-1500
fax: 202-628-1509
www.aibs.org

American Zoo and Aquarium Association
8403 Colesville Road, Suite 710
Silver Spring, MD 20910-3314
phone: 301-562-0777
fax: 301-562-0888
email: generalinquiry@aza.org
www.aza.org

Aquaculture Association of Canada
16 Lobster Lane
St. Andrews, New Brunswick
Canada E3B 3T6
phone: 506-529-4766
fax: 506-529-4609
www.aquacultureassociation.ca

Human Dolphin Institute
6505 Sunset Avenue, Unit B
Panama City Beach, FL 32408
phone: 800-207-2780
fax: 850-230-1873
email: info@human-dolphin.org
www.human-dolphin.org

Institute for Marine Mammal Studies
Marine Life Oceanarium
P.O. Box 4078
Gulfport, MS 39502-4078
phone: 228-864-2511
fax: 228-863-3673
email: info@imms.org
www.imms.org

International Association for Aquatic Animal Medicine
The Florida Aquarium
701 Channelside Drive
Tampa, FL 33602
www.iaaam.org

International Association of Fish and Wildlife Agencies
(IAFWA)
444 North Capitol Street, NW, Suite 544
Washington, DC 20001
phone: 202-624-7890
fax: 202-624-7891
email: iafwa@sso.org
www.iafwa.org

International Marine Animal Trainers Association
(IMATA)
1200 South Lake Shore Drive
Chicago, IL 60605
www.imata.org

National Aquarium in Baltimore
501 East Pratt Street
Baltimore, MD 21202
phone: 410-576-3800
www.aqua.org

National Fisheries Institute
7918 Jones Branch Drive, Suite 700
McLean, VA 22102
phone: 703-524-8880
fax: 703-524-4619
email: tressler@nfi.org
www.nfi.org

National Marine Fisheries Service
National Oceanic and Atmospheric Administration
NOAA Fisheries
1315 East West Highway, SSMC3
Silver Spring, MD 20910
email: cyberfish@noaa.gov
www.nmfs.noaa.gov

Ontario Commercial Fisheries' Association
45 James Street, P.O. Box 2129
Blenheim, Ontario
Canada N0P 1A0
phone: 519-676-0488
fax: 519-676-0944
email: ocfa@ocfa.on.ca
www.ocfa.on.ca

Pacific Fishery Management Council
7700 NE Ambassador Place, Suite 200
Portland, OR 97220-1384
phone: 503-820-2280
fax: 503-820-2299
email: pfmc.comments@noaa.gov
www.pcouncil.org

World Aquaculture Society (WAS)
143 J. M. Parker Coliseum
Louisiana State University
Baton Rouge, LA 70803
phone: 225-578-3137
fax: 225-578-3493
www.was.org

World Wildlife Fund
1250 24th Street, NW
Washington, DC 20037
phone: 202-293-4800
email: piresponse@wwfus.org
www.worldwildlife.org

Internet Sites

Animal Training at Sea World
www.seaworld.org/animal_training/attraining.html

Alliance of Marine Mammal Parks and Aquariums
www-biology.ucsc.edu/alliance

Dolphin Research Center
www.dolphins.org

Society for Marine Mammalogy
www.pegasus.cc.ucf.edu/~smm/home.html

Virginia Marine Science Museum
www.vmsm.com

Most aquariums have job listings on their websites, as does the American Zoo and Aquarium Association: www.aza.org/JobListings/

Profile

AQUARIST
Andy Dehart

"My interest in this field began when I was four years old," says Andy Dehart, currently the animal care center manager at the National Aquarium in Baltimore. That was when he first experienced the water. He was on a Caribbean trip when "my dad basically put me into the water, kicking and screaming, with a mask, fins, and snorkel on." But Dehart quickly took to the water and later his father had to "physically pull me out."

Dehart learned the basics of snorkeling that year and became a certified diver at age fifteen. "This passion has continued," he says. "There
was no doubt that I wanted to be a marine biologist. I began volunteering at the aquarium when I was a sophomore in high school, and
worked on my first research team with Earthwatch, tagging sharks in
the Bahamas, when I was sixteen." This is typical, Dehart says: most
people enter this career because of their interest in the field.

As animal care center manager, Dehart uses his skills as an aquarist in overseeing the "offsite quarantine facility where ninety percent
of our new animals come to go through medical treatments and observation before they are put on display." He uses people-management
skills in overseeing the aquarist staff who carry out husbandry duties
and administrative skills in managing the budget and the collecting
programs.

En route to this job, Dehart held two unpaid positions, an aquarist
internship and a volunteer aquarist position, as well as a paid seasonal
position as an aquarist aide. His first full-time paid position was as an
aquarist. He later became a senior aquarist before being promoted to
manager. He hopes to one day become an aquarium curator and manage the entire department.

"This long progression of steps is the norm to get a full-time aquarist position," he says. "Much of what you need to know to work in the
aquarium industry is not taught in school." The required educational
background for the career is a bachelor's in science—general biology,
chemistry, conservation, or marine biology. "A science degree shows
that you understand the scientific method and that you have the math-
ematical and problem-solving skills to stay current in this ever-
changing field." In addition, scuba certification is essential. "Scuba
diving is a skill that you will need to do the job, and it demonstrates a
continued interest in the aquatic environment."

Internships and volunteer work are key to getting a job. Most
internships are unpaid because aquariums are usually non-profit.
Volunteer work can go on concurrently with schooling, and Dehart
recommends it as the single best way to learn the work and get a full-
time job.

Describing a typical day at work is hard. "Personally, I feel that
one of the best aspects about this job is that there really is no typical
day," Dehart says. "Because you are dealing with animals, no two days
are the same." What there is of a daily routine is based on the structure

of the fishes department at the Baltimore aquarium. Each of the ten aquarists there maintains one gallery and is accountable for day-to-day gallery operations. As in a museum, each gallery contains a series of exhibits, often with a theme such as local Maryland habitats or the Pacific Northwest. Aquarists usually specialize in the particular habitat they maintain, but they must also be able to cover for other staff on weekends and days off.

Dehart arrives at work at seven-thirty and checks his schedule, noting whether he needs to cover another gallery that day. Then he inspects the gallery, or galleries, for which he is responsible. He checks the health of the animals, the functioning of the life support system, and the cleanliness of the galley. He records the temperature and the filter pressure, and, if necessary, takes water samples. He also begins thawing food for the daily feeding and checks email and other correspondence. He takes care of necessary water changes, chemical additions, or tank cleaning, and then prepares the food and feeds the animals. It is important that he record these feedings—quantity and so forth—and other tasks in the record book. If he is lucky, his day ends at four.

Some tasks are impossible to schedule into a routine. These include the "annual physicals on large display animals, such as the sharks; planning and designing new exhibits; ordering new animals for an exhibit; and participating in various collecting trips." He also administers medical treatments for sick or diseased animals; designs, builds, and plumbs new life support systems; fixes leaks or damaged life support equipment; and makes saltwater for the marine exhibits. At different times, Dehart performs presentation feedings, attends various departmental meetings, and trains interns and volunteers.

Tasks that he considers unpleasant include cleaning galleries and scrubbing and mopping the food preparation area. But, he says, "the main drawback to this profession is the pay. But, then again, can you imagine how competitive this field would be if it was this fun *and* it made you wealthy? Aquarists and marine biologists do what they do and love it because they have a passion for the aquatic environment and the creatures that it holds."

The hours are another problem: "It is not a nine-to-five job. When new animals are being shipped in or an exhibit is being renovated or when you are on a collecting trip it is not uncommon to work very long hours," he says. "When I helped open the aquarium at the Henry Doorly Zoo in Nebraska, we routinely worked seventy- or eighty-hour weeks during the last few months of construction. It was exhausting, but I experienced some of the most rewarding times in my career."

Because the work is with live animals, staff are needed on weekends and holidays. In the Baltimore aquarium rotation system, aquarists take turns working holidays and work one weekend every three weeks. Some institutions use a split week with half of the staff working from Sunday to Thursday and the other half from Tuesday to Saturday.

These drawbacks, however, do not daunt Dehart. "In any given year I will spend a number of days getting to literally hold a ten-foot lemon shark in my arms while we give it a physical, scuba dive in the Bahamas to collect fish in hand nets, or observe an octopus learn a new trained behavior," he enthuses. "These experiences are priceless. Many of these events are things that other people only dream of doing. It is a very active job that keeps you moving and interacting."

The useful personality traits in this work are varied, Dehart notes: "Anyone interested in this field needs to be able to work in a team setting and also be self-motivated to work independently. A professional aquarist will be called upon to do both on a daily basis." A strong love of animals is essential because the job can be very dirty and physically demanding. "I have seen many an intern who was very interested in becoming an aquarist end up being quite squeamish when it was time to get their hands dirty with blood and guts cutting up the food for the animals."

Technology is vital to his work. "The basic skills of email, using the Internet, and word processing are vital to keeping records and correspondence with other institutions," he notes. Additionally, "aquarium science is a very technical field. Much of the life support systems and engineering requires basic technical skills and understanding."

Dehart says that this is a job with a good future, although the boom in aquarium development of the 1990s and early 2000s has begun to slow as some markets are becoming saturated. But he notes that new aquariums continue to open and some existing aquariums are expanding their exhibits and programs. With each new aquarium or expansion, new techniques and technologies are developed.

He cautions, however, that "the job market is very competitive. Obviously, this is a very specialized job, and job openings are not very frequent at many institutions. When jobs are available there is a clear trend to hire from within for entry-level positions. People coming out of that institution's intern or volunteer program usually fill these positions."

Dehart's advice to individuals interested in aquarist work is to get involved in marine animals early and be willing to volunteer and intern. In addition to work experience, this can help beginners determine whether they want to pursue this type of work. "It is often very difficult to work for free or very low pay," he says, "but it is essential to gain the basic knowledge needed to apply for a biological position at a public aquarium." An additional benefit is that "these programs let the management observe what type of worker the applicant is." His final piece of advice is to run an aquarium at home. "Many of the life support and biological principles that are used in a small home tank are just magnified within the public aquarium. Getting the background knowledge through the hobby puts a candidate that much further ahead."

If Dehart did not love his work, he would not be able to state so unequivocally that "I have been in this field for fifteen years and have never questioned my career choice. There is something new every day, and the field is constantly growing. There are always new techniques or technologies to learn about."

Profile

MARINE LIFE FISHERMAN
Forrest Young

"I can't remember a time when I was not interested in animals," says Forrest Young. "Growing up on the edge of a small town meant that I spent almost every free waking moment exploring the nearby woods." Young also remembers very distinctly the first aquarium he ever visited, even though he was quite young at the time.

Although Young prefers to call himself a "marine life fisherman," the work he does is often categorized under the label of marine collector. Young's academic background includes earning a bachelor of science and a master's degree, his study for his master's focused on the ecology of aquatic insects in northeastern Pennsylvania. He was involved with larger aquatic life in his first job, however, when he worked as a research officer for a private aquaculture corporation. While working a five-day week, Young soon got into a rhythm of earning money "to make ends meet" by catching fish on the weekend for someone who supplied private aquariums. He was soon approached directly by an aquarium to provide fish.

At that point, Young evaluated his situation and realized that he had no chance of moving upward in his weekday job. Additionally, he was earning more for his weekend work than he did during the week. So he decided to strike out on his own, starting up his own business in 1979. In four years he was able to hire his first employee. Later that year he incorporated the business, and Dynasty Marine Associates was born. He has not looked back or markedly changed the structure of his business in the twenty-some years since then.

Says Young, "The plan is there is no plan." He explains that on the days that they go to sea to capture animals, they have a certain species in mind. If, for any reason, that animal is not available, they may have to change directions by midday. This means that they always need several contingency plans for each day. With his wealth of experience in this work, Young says that he can plan the approximate length of a day's work, because he knows about how long it takes to acquire a specific type and number of marine species. That is, if all goes according to his calculations.

Staffing needs change, but Dynasty Marine currently has eleven full-time staff and three part-time staff. The senior staff at Dynasty work on average a six-day work week. During acquisition times, Young says, they work longer—usually about seventy hours a week. As owner, Young himself spends almost that amount of time just on office and organizational work. He has many responsibilities in addition to harvesting marine animals. "My duties," he says, "involve a whole variety of work, from taking out the trash to hiring and firing staff."

Essential requirements for this work include a basic understanding of the life sciences, which is gained, says Young, from "a university degree in biology or the life sciences." In these courses students also gain "a basic understanding of bacteriology, physiology, endocrinology, and animal behavior." Other very important knowledge comes from studying chemistry and mathematics; marine collectors need to be able to calculate the volume of a tank and dosages of medications and foods.

Understanding animal behavior is most essential, however. "Knowing animal behavior is very, very important in the job," Young says. "Recognizing when animals are stressed, for example, is essential. We need to know this to capture them and keep them alive for delivery. Understanding their feeding behavior and the whole range of responses that helps predict their behavior can make workers more effective in going after the quarry. For example, when we capture fish by hook and line, the way we capture sharks, there is a strong behavioral response—each fish has a reciprocal response to the bait. We need to understand and anticipate this response to capture them with a minimal amount of stress for the fish." Young adds that individuals who begin work with these basic understandings respond much more quickly to specific on-the-job training.

However, Young's work does not end with the capture of the aquatic species. He explains that the next challenge is transporting them; the animals he delivers must arrive alive and healthy. Dynasty Marine uses three methods of transportation for the captured animals. The least preferred method of transportation, air cargo on a passenger flight, may be subject to the vagaries of weather and other factors and is occasionally unreliable. When the company uses this method, it carefully researches whether flights are on time or whether other factors may be affecting flight scheduling. If there is a potential delay, the aquatic life may need to be packed in a larger amount of water. Young's preferred method for delivery in the continental United States is by ground transportation, using Dynasty's own trailer. This method is more predictable, it is easier to pack more water, and the survival rate is almost a hundred percent. If Dynasty has a large international shipment, they use a third method of transportation: chartering an aircraft.

Young cites a number of personality traits that are essential for his work. "Individuals must be willing to work in conditions that have a certain amount of adversity," Young says. "It may be dangerous because of the type of fish that are around or they may need to go into dirty water." Also important is "a willingness to work long hours and to be relatively outgoing." He concludes with what some would consider negative aspects of the work: "People must also not be afraid to get their hands dirty or wet and not mind the smell of fish."

His advice to people who want to get into this type of work is to gain experience that demonstrates their ability to take the initiative and work well as part of a team. For his own staff, for example, Young looks for recommendations from professors about students who have completed independent research and have experience with hands-on fieldwork, because a high degree of initiative is essential in this work. Young also looks for people with a solid history of participation in team sports.

Although Young loves his work, he says wryly, "It would be nice to have more stability." He depends upon the aquarium business for his work, which is in turn dependent on consumer demand. The amount of work, he says, "is strictly on-demand. We supply aquariums with display animals and work to fill specific orders from clients.

Our work totally reflects the demand of clients for animals." Young says that he noted a significant downward trend for budgets of both public and private aquariums after September 11, 2001. Additionally, the building of private aquariums has been plateauing in the United States. "There are a relatively finite number of institutions," he notes, adding that he may need to revise his business plans in the future.

Nonetheless, Young takes great satisfaction from supplying live animals to aquariums. He loves collecting because, as he says: "I have the freedom to pursue my personal interests during work hours. There is an interplay between my personal and work goals."

Chapter 6

Reptiles and Amphibians

Can I unmoved see thee dying
On a log,
Expiring frog!

Charles Dickens

Herpetology is the field of study that encompasses reptiles and amphibians. The basic academic field of study for this work is biology, the study of living organisms. Zoology, a branch of biology, is the scientific study of animals that examines details such as their structure and distribution. Herpetology is in turn a branch of zoology.

Anyone entering this field must have a great interest in reptiles and amphibians, as well as a general concern for animals. Reptiles are cold-blooded, air-breathing vertebrates; they include snakes, lizards, crocodiles, alligators, turtles, and tortoises. Amphibians are also cold-blooded but can live both on land and in water; they include frogs, toads, newts, and salamanders.

Work involving reptiles and amphibians is quite diverse, as are the work settings. The background needed for such work is just as diverse. Some jobs require no academic studies, but experience with one or more species; others require an advanced degree.

"Herpetology" can be an umbrella title that covers any work with reptiles and amphibians, instead of an actual description of a specific type of work. Many of the jobs that deal with reptiles and amphibians are listed for herpetologists or fall under herpetology. This chapter describes the different types of herpetology work in greater detail.

HERPETOLOGIST

Salary Range: Depends on job, geographic location, and
employer. Starting pay is around $15,000 to $30,000 a
year (see individual positions for more details).

Educational Requirements: Varies from no studies, but with
experience, to a bachelor's degree in biology or a master's in herpetology. A doctorate is required for research,
university teaching, and specialist positions.

Employment Outlook: The job market is small, and competition for jobs is intense.

Under the general classification of "herpetologist" are people who
have advanced academic degrees and research experience, people who
work with reptiles and amphibians for a living but have not studied
science, and people whose interest in and pursuit of reptiles and
amphibians is simply a pleasurable pastime. Herpetologists find work
as teachers; in zoos, reptile parks, and crocodile farms; in museums;
and in state conservation agencies. Some also work as writers or photographers or develop their own reptile parks.

The academic requirements for professional herpetological positions are dependent upon the specific type of work involved, but most
positions requiring an academic background begin with the general
requirement of a biology degree. Only in general zoo work, in some
settings, is a degree not essential. Here, experience with reptiles or
amphibians is more important; those who have or have had these creatures as pets will have an edge in getting general zoo jobs. No college
or university offers a major in herpetology at the undergraduate or
graduate level; students interested in herpetology usually major in the
biological sciences, taking any specific herpetology courses that are
offered. Knowledge learned about the biology of animals then can be
applied to an individual study of amphibians and reptiles. Herpetology students should also take other courses, such as computer studies,
statistics, chemistry, writing, and foreign languages.

Graduate programs allow students to get into advanced studies
of a specific aspect of herpetology. Sometimes a little-known college
or university will have an outstanding herpetologist with a particular specialty on its faculty. These herpetologists write articles in the
major herpetological journals—*Copeia, Journal of Herpetology,* and
Herpetologica. Read current issues of these journals to find out who is

studying different aspects of herpetology and where these specialists teach.

Herpetology is divided into two fields. Pure, or basic, herpetology is simply the study of reptiles and amphibians in order to gather data such as habitats and breeding habits. Applied herpetology uses the knowledge accumulated by pure herpetologists to deal with specific problems or circumstances faced by reptiles and amphibians.

Pure Herpetology

Most herpetologists are involved in research on amphibians and reptiles, a function of pure herpetology. Much of this research takes place outdoors, often in remote areas, but some is carried on in laboratories or at farms and parks that have captive reptiles. The herpetologists study how these animals behave and why (their ethobiology), where they live and why (their ecology), how their bodies are structured (their anatomy) and how they function (their physiology), what they eat (their diet), and how they relate to creatures of previous eras (their paleontology). Scientific books, journals, and textbooks publish the results of this research.

In the last ten to twenty years, scientists have been particularly alarmed by a general decline in frog populations and the appearance of malformations within them. Frogs are very sensitive to the environment and, since they are amphibians, live both on land and in water. When they find that a frog species is experiencing problems, scientists speculate not only about the cause and the possible loss of a species, but also about how other species might be affected, including, ultimately, humans.

Taxonomy is a specialization within pure herpetology. A taxonomist researches the relationships among the various species of reptiles and amphibians, developing a framework that explains these relationships. In the process, taxonomists usually accumulate information about the distribution, or biogeography, of various species.

Applied Herpetology

People who work in applied herpetology use the information gathered by the pure herpetologists for practical applications. Some applied herpetologists maintain reptiles in captivity in places such as zoos or reptile parks. They must know the life histories of the animals to keep them in conditions that approximate their natural environment and provide them with the appropriate food.

Positions for Herpetologists

The requirements and pay for each job in herpetology depend upon the work setting. The most common settings are colleges and universities, museums, and zoological parks. Other positions might be found in wildlife management. Entrepreneurs, writers, photographers, and filmmakers also may work with reptiles and amphibians.

Colleges and Universities. By far the greatest numbers of herpetologists work in colleges and universities as professors. Universities require a doctorate for professors, although some smaller institutions may hire teachers who have only a master's degree. Few institutions have many courses specifically in herpetology, so a herpetologist mostly teaches more general biology courses, including introductory biology, anatomy, and ecology. The salary range for professors is from $30,000 to $80,000, depending upon the experience of the individual and the institution.

As with any job, teaching has both positive and negative aspects and difficulties to be overcome over the course of a career. Robin Andrews, the herpetologist profiled on page 123, notes, "I think the two most difficult aspects of the job for new academics are, number one, you can't work with one project until it is done and then start another. You must be able to multitask all of the time. Number two, research goals can have really delayed gratification. A paper you think has been completed comes back from a journal with reviewer's suggestions for improvement, and these may be substantial. When you have finally resolved these problems, then the editor wants more revisions. Then you wait even longer for your paper to be published. I have become used to the pattern of academic life, but some folks don't and leave academia either voluntarily or because they don't get tenure."

Some universities have positions as research or laboratory assistants that do not require a doctorate. The assistants may study herpetology while working and have access to excellent libraries and research equipment. The salary range for full-time research or laboratory assistants is from $17,000 to $35,000.

Museums. Museums have several types of jobs for herpetologists. Curators or scientists usually work full-time in research and require a doctorate in biology. Some museums are associated with universities, and in these situations the jobs of professor and curator may be combined; one person teaches and also researches for the museum, possibly on a half-time basis for each job. The salary range for museum curators or scientists is from $30,000 to $80,000, depending upon experience.

Large museums employ collection managers, who care for preserved amphibians and reptiles by cataloging and keeping records of the museum's specimens. They also make these specimens available for research. These jobs require a master's degree in biology or museum studies. The salary range for collection managers is $18,000 to $45,000.

Lower-level positions also exist for museum assistants. These may be part-time jobs for students, especially if the museum is affiliated with a university. The full-time positions require a bachelor's degree, and the salary range is from $12,000 to $18,000.

Zoological Parks. Zoological parks have different levels of positions available. Zoo curators and zoo supervisors hold managerial positions, and they may not deal directly with the animals on a regular basis. These positions usually require a master's degree in biology. The salary range for curators and supervisors is $30,000 to $50,000.

Most jobs for zookeepers require at least a bachelor's degree in biology; some require a master's degree. Zookeepers are responsible for the primary care of the animals in their charge; it's their job to feed, clean, and maintain them. A major reason reptiles and amphibians are kept in captivity is to educate the public, so zookeepers may need to make educational presentations to groups. Some zoos hire individuals who care for the animals under supervision. These positions do not require a degree, but experience with reptiles and amphibians as pets is very important. The salary range for zookeepers is $15,000 to $25,000. (For more information about curators and zookeepers, see Chapter 9. Also see the zookeeper/reptile zoo owner profile on page 126 and the elephant handler profile on page 169.)

Large zoos may have positions available solely for educators, who organize educational programs. They may also present programs or speak to various local organizations. These jobs usually require a master's degree. Some of the larger zoos also hire researchers, who do work similar to the research that takes place in a university or museum; these jobs require a doctorate.

Wildlife Management. State governments and the federal government employ a few herpetologists in wildlife management positions. Some of these jobs require fieldwork; others involve both field research and researching and drafting regulations. Some private conservation organizations offer similar jobs. The minimum degree for these jobs is a bachelor's, most likely in wildlife management, but often a master's or doctorate in biology is required. Pay varies quite a lot and is dependent upon the organization, the specific requirements of each job, and the location. (For more information on work in wildlife management, see Chapter 7.)

Entrepreneurial Jobs. Some entrepreneurs start their own businesses breeding and selling amphibians and reptiles; others produce related merchandise or publications. A limited number of people sell frog legs as a delicacy. Others extract, or milk, snake venom for use as an antivenin or for research; this is a very exacting, highly skilled job. The money earned by entrepreneurs varies widely.

Writing, Photography, and Films. People with the knowledge, interest, and talent can make a living writing books and magazine articles about various herpetological subjects. Others photograph amphibians and reptiles, selling their pictures to publishers. Nature films have grown more popular with the increase in TV channels and a broader interest in nature and conservation; some people make a living creating and producing films about reptiles and amphibians. The pay varies extensively, depending on the individual project.

RESOURCES

American Society of Ichthyologists and Herpetologists
Florida International University
Biological Sciences
11200 SW 8th Street
Miami, FL 33199
phone: 305-348-1235
fax: 305-348-1986
e-mail: asih@fiu.edu
www.asih.org

Global Gecko Association (GGA)
1155 Cameron Cove Circle
Leeds, AL 35094
www.gekkota.com

Herpetologist's League
www.inhs.uiuc.edu
Montreal Herpetological Association
www.montreal-herp.org

Society for the Study of Amphibians and Reptiles
P.O. Box 253
Marceline, MO 64658-0253
www.ssarherps.org

Profile

HERPETOLOGIST AND UNIVERSITY PROFESSOR
Robin Andrews

"I had no idea that a love of nature could be turned into a job until I was in college," says Robin Andrews. Andrews, an academic who teaches and researches in the biology department at Virginia Tech, grew up with a love of natural history and the outdoors. "As a child," she says, "I cultivated plants and raised many pets, including tropical fish, birds, guppies, toads, snakes, salamanders, and a dog."

Andrews, who has degrees from the University of Kansas, Harvard, and the University of Minnesota, worked in a natural history museum during her undergraduate years, helping the scientists with their research. Initially, she majored in entomology, the study of insects. She was well on her way to a doctorate in entomology when a chance remark from a professor changed her course of study and her future research emphasis. During a field course in Costa Rica, her professor noted a lizard alongside the rainforest path and speculated how its predatory behavior would affect the coloration and behavior of the insects that it ate. Andrews became interested in the dietary habits of these insectivorous lizards and returned from a year of study in Costa Rica with a thesis on lizards and their interactions with insects. This marked her shift from entomology to vertebrate biology, with a focus on reptiles.

In her current job, she spends fifty percent of her time teaching and fifty percent in research. She conducts original research, focusing on ecology and evolution, and publishes papers describing the results. Her job also includes "writing grant proposals to obtain funding for her laboratory and training graduate students." She conducts field and laboratory studies on spiny and tree lizards and laboratory studies on the veiled chameleon. Locally, the species she studies is the eastern fence lizard, *Sceloporus undulatus*; she has also studied other species in the genus *Sceloporus* in Mexico and Arizona.

She currently has three students in her laboratory: one Ph.D. candidate, one master's candidate, and one undergraduate. Prospective graduate students usually apply to institutions based on a professor's research interests, which they've learned about from reading his or her published papers. In Andrews's case, students were accepted into her laboratory because their research interests paralleled hers. She oversees their research, and they in turn assist in hers. The assistance they provide is based upon their individual strengths and interests; for example, the exceptional organizational skills of her current undergraduate student help the laboratory to function smoothly and keep experiments on schedule.

From May to September, when the lizards she studies are most active, Andrews and her students carry out research in the field and laboratory. "Each research season typically involves field studies in which I make behavioral observations and determine abundance, growth in size, and survival. I also collect gravid [pregnant] females to bring to the laboratory, where they will lay their eggs. My laboratory studies involve making observations on embryos at different times of development and under different controlled incubation conditions. Field and laboratory studies are synergistic: I learn the most when I combine information from the two. Other activities during this period include writing papers or grant proposals and advising students in the laboratory."

The academic year, from September to May, finds Andrews teaching one class a semester. "The class is usually large, with a hundred to a hundred and forty students, and is required by our majors. Right now I am teaching evolutionary biology at the sophomore level." She has taught this course for four years; some semesters she teaches a graduate-level course. Teaching involves preparing and giving lectures and exams, helping students enrolled in the course, and advising both undergraduate and graduate students. She also chairs the committee that evaluates applications for departmental graduate programs and is involved with other departmental administrative duties. Research continues during the academic year, because her chameleons breed year-round.

She also analyzes data and prepares manuscripts for publication. Publication is expected, she says; it shows that you are active in your discipline. Writing research papers has become one of the favorite parts of her job. "It is now the most creative process I am involved with," she says. "It's like a big puzzle to put everything together."

According to Andrews, the ideal preparation for this kind of academic teaching and research career is "a Ph.D. and often post-doctoral experience," and people typically get graduate degrees from several different institutions. "Community and some four-year colleges hire people with master's degrees," she says, "but these jobs are usually centered on teaching, with a minor research component."

A typical career path in her field, says Andrews, usually involves a sequence of positions, beginning with work as a post-doctoral fellow. The first academic post is that of nontenured assistant professor. This leads to the position of associate professor with tenure, and then, finally, professor with tenure.

Andrews speaks positively about the role of modern technology in her work, which she says "has made my job much more efficient and fun. For example, I can locate and access publications without leaving my desk. I go to the library much less often now. I can easily collaborate on papers and books with colleagues around the world. Communication is immediate. Word processing makes writing much easier."

Top among the skills required for her job is the scientific expertise that she uses in her teaching and research. This expertise includes the knowledge she gained from her education and her research while being guided as a student, the techniques she has learned in her career, and the ability to ask novel questions that point in a new direction of research. Her expertise is constantly stimulated and expanded by communication with people at different levels of knowledge—high school students, her undergraduate and graduate students, and her peers. Other skills include the use of statistics and many different kinds of computer software. Helpful personality traits for this type of career, according to Andrews, are perseverance and attention to detail.

Andrews considers the outlook for this type of job good: "Educators will always have jobs, and science-related careers are especially good right now." Her advice to those interested in this type of career is to "excel academically and take advantage of every opportunity to get research experience." Jobs in the field are advertised nationally in publications such as *Science* and the *Chronicle of Higher Education*. She cautions that people should apply only for positions for which they are truly qualified, since high-profile jobs may have hundreds of applicants.

Because of the split between teaching and research, Andrews says that her working conditions vary. During the summer, she spends at least a few hours a day with animals, but somewhat less during the rest of the year. However, she loves the combination of teaching and researching. "The best part of my job is that I have freedom to choose the kind of research that I will conduct and the specific content of my lectures. While the performance standards are high in both of these areas, I decide how to meet these standards. I also like being part of a group of educators with the common goal of providing an excellent education to our students." After almost thirty years in this career, she says, "I really can't define any part of my job that I don't like."

Profile

ZOOKEEPER AND REPTILE ZOO OWNER
Paul "Little Ray" Goulet

"I've been interested in reptiles ever since I was old enough to understand that I would never see a real dinosaur," says Paul "Little Ray" Goulet, zookeeper and owner of Little Ray's Reptile Zoo in Ottawa, Ontario. Goulet "fell into" this work after an experience assisting seventh-grade science classes. One day the teachers asked him to bring some of his reptile pets to school. "The rest," as he says, "is history."

In 1995, Goulet established Little Ray's Reptile Adventure, a traveling educational show. Initially, his focus was on schools. He took his reptiles to various classrooms to complement his presentation about exotic and indigenous reptile species. Soon, he expanded his audience, adding presentations to scout troops, birthday parties, corporate events, malls, fairs, and retirement centers. He also started traveling to cities where people do not have access to any animal education, building a mini zoo where guests can visit the display, see the educational presentations, and touch and hold different creatures from around the globe. In the beginning, he balanced his reptile work with a part-time job as a commercial lending manager at a bank. As soon as he felt that he could do zookeeping full-time, he left the bank and never looked back.

The opening of the permanent reptile zoo in 2000 again expanded the audience for Goulet's more than four hundred reptiles. Although people can wander through the zoo looking at the reptiles and insects, the highlight of any visit is the dynamic presentation given by Goulet or one of his staff. The presentation is fun, educational, and interactive, appealing to people of all ages. Learning more about these rarely seen species helps to debunk some commonly held myths, Goulet says. The zoo's regular staff of about seven expands to about thirty in the summer to handle the greater influx of visitors.

Although Goulet went to traditional zoos as a child, the only thing he really liked about them was seeing the animals. Even then he hated seeing animals in cages or small enclosures. "We do things differently than most zoos," he notes. "I wanted to have the most hands-on, interactive zoo that anyone could go to."

Goulet cannot overemphasize the educational mandate of his zoo. He strongly believes in conservation of animal resources and knows that education is the key to helping others understand the necessity of conservation. He is quick to point out that Little Ray's does not import any animals for the zoo, but is instead a reptile rescue organization. Most of the reptiles in his zoo are unwanted pets; others are animals from local breeders and other zoos. Today, Little Ray's is the largest reptile zoo in Canada.

As the head curator at the zoo, Goulet is "directly responsible for the care and maintenance of every single animal under our care. I also play a large role in our education programming." He spends a great deal of time on the job overseeing the other keepers and setting and maintaining guidelines for animal care. He estimates that about fifty to seventy percent of his time is spent with the animals.

Goulet underscores the role that his wife Sheri has had in the zoo's success. In fact, the advice that he offers to any man interested in a career like his is: "If you want to be successful doing educational programs with reptiles and open your own reptile zoo, you need to have a woman who will support you." Although Sheri was not enthusiastic about reptiles when he met her, he says that her work at the zoo is indispensable to its success. She looks after administrative aspects of the zoo—bookings, staffing, and so forth—and also cares for the venomous snakes, insects, and arachnids. Between them, the Goulets handle the most dangerous work at the zoo.

The excellence of Little Ray's educational program has brought recognition at home and abroad, recognition that has led to a zoo consulting sideline. In the past year, Little Ray's staff has assisted zoological facilities in India and Singapore in designing and setting up their own educational programs.

Although he cannot describe a typical day's work—he "does different things on different days"—some tasks must be performed every day. Goulet's daily responsibilities include feeding the animals, cleaning the animal enclosures, and providing any necessary medical care. "There are always one or two animals that require medical care on a daily basis," he says. "In addition, because we focus so much on education, I never pass up an opportunity to talk with and teach the public."

The best background for persons wanting to do zookeeping work, Goulet says, is experience. Helpful experience can be gained from volunteering at a zoo or vet clinic. "The more experience people have in dealing directly with animals, the better their chances of getting hired full-time at any zoo," he says. Also important is a degree in an animal-related subject such as biology or zoology. In college Goulet studied science, majoring in geographical information systems and fitting as many zoological courses as he could into his schedule; he is still three courses short of a bachelor's degree, which he intends to complete soon. He seriously values a university education, but says, "By far I believe that experience is the best learning tool." When Goulet hires new keepers, he also looks for personable, enthusiastic people. "Everyone that works here deals with the public in some way or another," he says, "so we are all very outgoing people. I'd have to say that personality and basic common sense will take you far in this industry."

Goulet admits that not all zoos live up to their mission. "The thing that irritates me the most about the industry is all the politics that are involved with large zoos," he says emphatically. "Although the intention is to protect the animals—usually—sometimes the best interests of the animals are the last thing that are considered."

He has been fortunate in his own work, however. "I love being a zookeeper so much that I built my own zoo," he declares. "I love just about everything I do on a daily basis."

Chapter 7

Wild Animals

All animals, except man, know that the
principal business of life is to enjoy it—and
they do enjoy it as much as man and other
circumstances will allow.
                Samuel Butler, *The Way of All Flesh*

Although some jobs involving native North American wildlife are found in zoos, sanctuaries, or preserves, most such work takes place in the animals' natural habitats. Professionals who work with animals in the wild are involved in protecting these habitats and preserving species as well as individual animals. Some of the most cutting-edge work with animals is done in their natural habitats. Health researchers have recently begun to study animals in the wild to help prevent and avoid illness. This work has even spawned a new branch of science—zoopharmacognosy, the study of how animals self-medicate—that is still in its infancy.

Federal, state, and provincial government agencies generally consider native wildlife to be a natural resource that should be preserved and managed for the benefit of humans and have enacted many wildlife management laws. The U.S. Fish and Wildlife Services operates more than 540 wildlife refuges, which operate specifically to shelter endangered wildlife and plant species. Many also are used for wildfowl breeding and nesting.

The lure of working with wild animals in their natural state is sometimes romanticized; the actual work can often be quite demanding. Some of it may take place in remote locations with less-than-comfortable conditions. But for those who love wild animals and do not find such circumstances a drawback, no work can compare.

Not all of the work takes place in remote areas, however. Many jobs involve educating the public about wildlife and the laws that relate to it and occur in nature centers and other indoor locations. Some may involve the lawmaking process itself, proposing or writing laws for legislators to introduce and consider. Other jobs are with private foundations or businesses concerned about the effects of their activities on wildlife and the environment.

If you are interested in this type of work, you should learn all that you can about animals and their habitats. Extensive training in the life sciences is imperative. College classes in the natural sciences—biology, zoology, and ecology—as well as science and math are good background courses for this type of work. Local organizations such as zoos or museums of natural history also may offer classes. Consider doing volunteer or part-time work or an internship to help you decide whether working with wild animals is the right career for you. Zoos, aquariums, parks, and wildlife centers and refuges all may have opportunities for volunteer or part-time work. Many zoos, conservation organizations, wetlands, and museums offer internships, which are valuable sources of information about animals and an excellent way to get to know professionals in the field, who can tell you about their work and give you advice.

This chapter looks at a number of positions involving work with wildlife, giving general information on the various types of jobs that are available in this field. The job titles are not as important as the job descriptions. Different employers often call jobs with essentially the same content by different names.

WILDLIFE MANAGEMENT

Nearly all of the jobs that deal with wildlife fall into the category of "wildlife management." Because most countries today consider their wildlife to be a natural resource that belongs to and should be preserved for the people, governments have developed policies and laws relating to the management of that resource. Government agencies oversee wildlife management, enforce wildlife policies and laws, and provide public education about animal species and conservation. Many developing or impoverished countries do not have the resources to adequately protect their wildlife, especially rare or endangered species, so some private organizations assist those countries with this work.

Wildlife management is, strictly speaking, an attempt by humans to ensure that various wildlife species serve the purposes mandated by law. All wildlife species—both game and nongame—are managed and the purposes may be ecological, recreational, commercial, or scientific. Wildlife management involves creating and managing habitats, overseeing hunting and fishing seasons and regulations, collecting data on various wildlife populations, and educating the public about wildlife and wildlife conservation.

A major function of wildlife management is to protect rare or endangered species. Such species often are endangered because of habitat destruction or changes to the environment by man. Conversely, some species have become so abundant that they are a threat to human property or life, especially as humans encroach into formerly wild, unsettled areas. Dealing with both situations is the responsibility of wildlife management professionals.

The types of wildlife management jobs available vary from location to location and are known by different names. Wildlife manager and wildlife researcher positions often fall under titles such as wildlife biologist or wildlife area supervisor. Wildlife law enforcement officials are sometimes called wildlife officers or game wardens. Because most wildlife management work involves public-relations skills, some positions deal almost entirely with this area; job titles include public information officer, wildlife education officer, publications editor, and public information specialist.

By far the greatest number of positions in wildlife management are at the state or provincial level of government. A few jobs can be found at the federal or county level. Some private organizations and companies also employ wildlife managers. Research your local government offices and organizations to learn about the jobs that are available. Look at job descriptions, not the titles, to find out exactly what work is going on where you live or in areas where you might want to live.

WILDLIFE BIOLOGIST

Salary Range: Federal government jobs average $26,000 a year with a bachelor's degree, $32,000 a year with a master's, and $37,000 or more with a doctorate. State or provincial government pay ranges from $22,000 to $30,000. Jobs in industry begin at around $38,000 a year.

Educational Requirements: A bachelor's degree is a must and a master's degree gives an edge. For research, university teaching, and many extension wildlife specialist positions, a doctorate is required.

Employment Outlook: Growing, especially as governments pay more attention to environmental concerns, but competition for jobs is intense.

Wildlife biologists work to conserve and manage wildlife and wildlife habitat. Their major concerns are the effects of humans on wildlife and, conversely, the effects of wildlife on humans. Wildlife biologists need to have a genuine concern about the environment, conservation, animals, and the outdoors; they must also have a keen desire to help wild animals.

Wildlife biologists work both indoors and outdoors. Outdoor work means working in all weather conditions and many different settings. It may involve trips or extended fieldwork that takes the biologist away from home for a long period of time. Indoor work may include time spent analyzing the results of fieldwork and preparing reports, working in a laboratory or a nature center, and teaching.

Some wildlife biologists study wildlife and their habitat. They may follow a particular species, collecting data about the age, size, and gender of individual animals and the distribution of the population. These biologists also examine the quality of the habitat and try to determine how weather, humans, and disease affect this population. They employ marking, trapping, aerial surveys, tracking by radio, and computer modeling in their work.

Other wildlife biologists focus on the effects of land use by humans on wildlife. They monitor the ecological effects of pollutants, such as sewage, acid rain, and pesticides. They may give workshops and seminars on land use as it affects wildlife or make recommendations to protect the ecological systems, suggesting ways to ameliorate the effects of land use on wildlife populations and habitat.

There are also wildlife biologists who focus on government policies relating to wildlife. They make recommendations on laws and regulations that protect wildlife, helping set policies on hunting, trapping, and planning and zoning for land use that is in harmony with wildlife.

Research and teaching are two other areas in which wildlife biologists find employment. Researchers study issues that relate to wildlife and their habitats. They apply for funding to support their research and report the results of their study either in scientific journals or in papers at conferences. They may also supervise student or technician researchers. Teachers provide instruction on the environment, biology, and wildlife. They often do research or consult for government or private companies in addition to the classes they teach.

A wildlife biologist also may find work in environmental consulting and environmental education, or as a park naturalist or park police officer. Again, the specific types of work that wildlife biologists find depend on their individual interests and skills.

Wildlife biologists need good problem-solving skills and the ability to interpret and analyze the data they collect. They should be physically fit and able to handle the challenges and dangers presented by working with large animals, if that is a focus of their work, and by time spent outdoors in various conditions. Communication skills are important for writing grant proposals, reports, and research summaries; speaking about land use issues; and explaining wildlife management goals in presentations to the public.

The hours of work may be irregular, especially when time is spent in the field. Advancement for wildlife biologists usually means work in management or administration, which is mainly indoor work with little direct animal contact, and often means moving to another location.

Experience is key in finding a job as a wildlife biologist; the field is very competitive. If you are interested in pursuing this career, you should do anything possible to get experience, including volunteering, internships, or short-term or part-time jobs. Additionally, work in the field during your studies will provide useful experience and helpful contacts. Getting hired may still be difficult, even though there is likely to be an increase in these jobs as governments seek to understand the effects of a growing human population on wildlife and its habitats. Many graduates of master's programs with extensive experience tell stories of the difficulties in landing a full-time wildlife biologist job. But these positions do exist; persistence and the ability to live on a shoestring budget during your search will most likely eventually pay off.

See profile on page 141.

WILDLIFE (BIOLOGICAL) TECHNOLOGIST OR TECHNICIAN

Salary Range: Seasonal, from $10 to $12.55 an hour.

Educational Requirements: Two-year degree, working on a bachelor's degree.

Employment Outlook: Available positions are highly competitive.

Wildlife technologists or technicians usually assist scientists who work in wildlife management or animal biology. They generally work in the field, providing technical support in research on animal populations or reproductive habits or settings, but they also may work in laboratory settings, offices for data entry or management, wildlife refuges, or even caves. These positions may be advertised as biological technicians or technologists, wildlife technologists, fish and wildlife officers, or fishery officers; read the job descriptions to see whether the work involves wildlife.

A technician's summer is mostly spent in the field collecting data. Fieldwork may involve examining the effects of hunting on wildlife populations or studying different bird species and their predators, nesting habits, and ranges. The work may include attaching tags or radio transmitters to animals in order to obtain data about habitat and migration patterns. Fieldwork often involves traveling long distances in four-wheel-drive vehicles over rough terrain. It may require difficult hiking while carrying awkward and heavy equipment. Wildlife technicians often need to be able to sterilize laboratory equipment in the wild to ensure that the samples collected are of high quality. They may be called upon to work day or night or both.

Wildlife technicians must be in good physical condition for fieldwork and able to tolerate different weather conditions, which may include extremes of temperatures and annoying insects. They need to be independent, highly motivated, enthusiastic, and well organized. Wildlife technicians also assist in analyzing data and preparing reports, and may enter data on a computer. Communication skills are important, as technicians may need to contact wildlife organizations, speak to local groups or visitors, and work with private landowners. Wildlife technicians must be able to work well with others, as their work sometimes requires being part of a larger team.

These positions are often seasonal and involve working for government departments. Some work is available with urban wildlife control companies, colleges and universities, environmental consulting firms, research companies, and utilities.

Doing actual fieldwork can help you pinpoint the area in which you should focus your studies. Seasonal positions are generally during the summers or hunting or fishing season. These positions can be especially helpful for students wishing to explore different options in this field. Additionally, working as a technician is a good way for a recent graduate to gain experience in pursuit of a full-time job.

WILDLIFE OFFICER

Salary Range: Varies, but generally ranges between $18,000 and $45,000.

Educational Requirements: Minimum two-year degree, but usually requires a bachelor's; courses in wildlife biology, wildlife management, environmental law enforcement, criminal justice, and related fields are important. Jobs that emphasize law enforcement may require a police officer degree.

Employment Outlook: Some job growth; over time, more positions will open because of retirement.

Wildlife officers must be knowledgeable about the wildlife and habitat where they are working—whether it is forest, water, or a combination of the two—and understand the life histories of the animals. They must know the details of the laws relating to hunting and fishing in their area.

Wildlife officers actually spend most of their time working not with the animals, but with the humans who are involved with wildlife—hunters, anglers, staff of local law enforcement agencies, and the general public. It is essential for wildlife officers to develop and maintain good working relationships with other officials and be able to relate well to other people in general. They need to have good communication skills, including public speaking.

Law enforcement is the primary focus of a wildlife officer. Such duties include checking the licenses carried by hunters and anglers, issuing citations, and arresting individuals who are caught hunting without a license or on private property. Another aspect of law enforcement is investigating accidents that involve hunters, animals, or both. Wildlife officers must know how to collect evidence to carry out this important responsibility. They must be able to testify in court, if necessary.

A wildlife officer's involvement in game management may include tracking the local population of a species and monitoring its health. Some wildlife officers are in charge of developing conservation programs for game species such as deer or waterfowl. These programs might eventually become part of state or provincial wildlife management plans; if so, the officer could be charged with maintaining and enforcing them. Conversely, officers may need to take steps to decrease an animal population if it is so large that it is threatened with starvation or is becoming a danger to humans. Officers might be involved in trying to solve problems related to animal diseases, such as rabies. At times they may be called upon to deal with large animals—coyotes, alligators, bears, wolves, mountain lions—that have wandered into populated areas. The officers' duty in such situations is usually to return these animals to the wild.

Wildlife officers should have training in first aid, firearms and firearm safety, and possibly boat safety. They need to be able to keep accurate records and prepare reports. Wildlife officers must be in good physical condition and able to work long hours during the peak hunting and fishing seasons.

WILDLIFE PUBLIC INFORMATION OFFICER

Salary Range: Between $29,000 and $38,000, depending upon location.

Educational Requirements: Bachelor's degree in communication, public relations, or natural sciences with experience in public relations.

Employment Outlook: Although some new positions may be created, the competition remains keen for available jobs.

A wildlife public information officer provides information to the public about wildlife issues, hunter safety, water safety, laws and regulations regarding wildlife, and a variety of other subjects. This information is often distributed through pamphlets, brochures, newsletters, or news releases.

An information officer's work usually includes writing and coordinating the publication and distribution of newsletters and magazines, as well as writing and maintaining relevant websites. These individuals also develop and staff exhibits and booths set up at conferences, trade shows, and similar events in order to provide information and generate publicity. Creating or supervising the development of educational videotapes and films for use in public presentations is often another duty of a public information officer.

Information officers must be knowledgeable about marketing and communication techniques used to present a positive image of an organization or government department while communicating useful and essential information to the public. Speaking skills are important—this work often involves public or community speeches or tours and sometimes actual classroom education. The ability to relate well to local and, perhaps, national media is essential, as is the ability to work well with others. Computer literacy and, usually, web proficiency are expected skills.

If the officer's work focuses on education, it may include training sessions and clinics for hunting, trapping, fishing, conservation, and environmental concerns.

Although most wildlife public information officer positions do not require actual work with wildlife, they do require knowledge of wildlife, wildlife management, and the laws relating to management. Hands-on wildlife work can include functions such as checking duck nest boxes, fishing nets, and hunting and fishing licenses; investigating fish kills and pollution; and, at times, making arrests.

WILDLIFE REHABILITATOR

Salary Range: Wide range, from stipend up to $30,000 per year with benefits.

Educational Requirements: College or university courses or a degree give an edge on the job and in finding work.

Employment Outlook: Some growth, but paying jobs are very competitive.

A wildlife rehabilitator is someone who cares for native wildlife that has been injured or inadvertently removed from a parent. The goal is to return the creature to its appropriate territory. This is a comparatively new field: although people have been fulfilling these functions on a completely ad hoc basis for many years, the first organizations designed to regulate and standardize this career date from only the early 1980s.

Many wildlife rehabilitators work from their homes, either as volunteers or on a contract basis, but they increasingly are finding jobs with rehabilitation centers that have the funding for staff. People who become wildlife rehabilitators come from varied backgrounds: veterinary science and technology, biology, or education.

Wildlife rehabilitator jobs can be very challenging, with the work varying from day to day and location to location. They can also be very repetitive, involving a daily routine of animal care. A rehabilitator captures and transports injured animals or birds, feeds both adults and young, assists with their therapies (such as fluid therapy), bandages them, and cleans cages. The work also involves interacting with other people: the rehabilitator may supervise paid staff and volunteers, give presentations to schools or organizations, and talk to people who call with problems and concerns relating to wild animals or the environment. Fund-raising may be involved in a rehabilitator's job, as well as maintaining databases about animals or members.

The work has many rewards, including helping relieve the suffering of animals. Contact with other staff and the public can be rewarding and positive aspects of the work.

A degree is not necessary for rehabilitation work, but the information learned in a degree program is very helpful on the job. A degree in biology gives graduates essential knowledge for providing good-quality care for animals. It also helps them understand the complex relationships among wildlife, humans, and the environment and gives an edge in a field that is quite competitive. No degrees specializing in wildlife rehabilitation are currently available; classes that relate to this field include anesthesiology, ecology, field techniques, raptor physiology, wildlife behavior, and wildlife management. Experience is very helpful in obtaining a paying position. You can gain experience by volunteering at a wildlife rehabilitation center or with a licensed rehabilitator. Seasonal positions and internships, either paid or unpaid, also can provide experience.

Wildlife rehabilitators need to be creative, realistic, and resourceful. They need to be self-motivated and interested in continuing to learn. Communication skills—both as a listener and a speaker—are essential as are high energy, willingness to work, and the ability to work as part of a team. Because the type of wildlife treated will vary considerably, it is essential that the rehabilitator is open to learning and can be trained. Wildlife rehabilitators also need a strong concern about wildlife, people, and the environment.

All wildlife rehabilitators in the United States must have both state and federal licenses or permits. In some locations, a permit from a local agency is necessary. Requirements differ from state to state, and rehabilitators are responsible for obtaining the correct license for the work they will be doing. Agencies granting these licenses are the U.S. Fish and Wildlife Service Migratory Bird Permit Section regional office and the state agency in charge of managing wildlife. The federal government is responsible for migratory birds and wildlife species that are endangered or threatened throughout the country. State agencies are responsible for species that do not migrate, as well as mammals, reptiles, and amphibians that are endangered or threatened in that state. Licensing in Canada is different in every province. Information on rehabilitating migratory birds can be gained from the provincial office of the Canadian Wildlife Service or Environment Canada.

Because the need for wildlife rehabilitators often arises from the interaction between humans and animals, the majority of rehabilitator jobs are located near areas with high human populations. Some of these centers are large, with a variety of jobs relating to wildlife rehabilitation.

Jobs can be found in both the private and public sectors. In the private sectors, the jobs are usually with nonprofit foundations and organizations such as the National Wildlife Rehabilitation Agency. Public-sector jobs can be found in some state, provincial, county, and city nature or environmental education facilities.

See profile on page 144.

RESOURCES

Canadian Public Relations Society
Suite 346, 4195 Dundas Street West
Toronto, Ontario
Canada M8X 1Y4
phone: 416-239-7034
fax: 416-239-1076
email: admin@cprs.ca
www.cprs.ca

Canadian Wildlife Federation (CWF)
350 Michael Cowpland Drive
Kanata, Ontario
Canada K2M 2W1
phone: 800-563-9453
fax: 613-599-4428
email: info@cwf-fcf.org
www.cwf-fcf.org

Federal Wildlife Officers Association
P.O. Box 646
Harrisburg, PA 17108
email: feedback@fwoa.org
www.fwoa.org

U.S. Fish and Wildlife Service
4040 North Fairfax Drive, Room 308
Arlington, VA 22203
phone: 800-344-9453
www.fws.gov

International Wildlife Rehabilitation Council (IWRC)
8080 Capwell Drive, Suite 240
Oakland, CA 94621
phone: 510-383-9090
email: office@iwrc-online.org
www.iwrc-online.org

National Wildlife Rehabilitators Association (NWRA)
14 North 7th Avenue
St. Cloud, MN 56303-4766
phone: 320-259-4086
email: nwra@nwrawildlife.org
www.nwrawildlife.org

North American Wildlife Enforcement Officers
Association
P.O. Box 22
Hollidaysburg, PA 16648
fax: 206-201-6953
email: naweoa@ureach.com
www.naweoa.org

Public Relations Society of America
33 Maiden Lane, 11th Floor
New York, NY 10038-5150
phone: 212-460-1400
fax: 212-995-0757
www.prsa.org

Student Conservation Association
P.O. Box 550
Charlestown, NH 03603-0550
phone: 603-543-1700
fax: 603-543-1828
www.sca-inc.org

Wildlife Disease Association
P.O. Box 1897
Lawrence, KS 66044-8897
phone: 785-843-1221
fax: 785-843-1274
www.wildlifedisease.org

Wildlife Management Institute
1146 19th Street, NW, Suite 700
Washington, DC 20036
phone: 202-371-1808
fax: 202-408-5059
www.wildlifemanagementinstitute.org

The Wildlife Society
5410 Grosvenor Lane, Suite 200
Bethesda, MD 20814-2144
phone: 301-897-9770
fax: 301-530-2471
email: tws@wildlife.org
www.wildlife.org

Internet Sites
Environmental Careers Organization
www.eco.org

Profile
WILDLIFE BIOLOGIST
Kim Poole

"It just seemed to happen," says Kim Poole about why he became a
wildlife biologist. As a youngster, Poole drew picture after picture of
animals, pictures that were carefully preserved by his grandmother. As
a teenager, he live-trapped mice in the meadows near his home and
did school projects about wildlife. At fifteen, he knew he wanted to get
a degree in wildlife biology.

A wildlife biologist, Poole says, researches or runs programs to
study or manage wildlife and their habitat. This could involve a wide
range of activities. He describes his work as "designing and conduct-

ing studies on a number of issues concerning wildlife, ranging from population estimates and surveys to habitat studies to determine which habitats animals require and how to mitigate impacts, such as from forestry, or enhance habitats." Studies on population ecology—distribution, migration, and reproduction—constitute a large part of his work. He also conducts environmental impact assessments in which he determines potential impacts and proposes measures to mitigate disturbances.

The ideal preparation for a job like his includes the basics, Poole says: a good schooling and experience. The minimum degree is a bachelor of science, but postgraduate work is preferred, and experience is invaluable. "There are a lot of people with biology degrees running around the country, but those with experience will often get the first crack at jobs. Unpaid experience is often needed to kick-start the system."

According to Poole, a wildlife biologist has to know "the fundamentals and principles of wildlife biology and management. You need to be able to think about what you see and why. Communication skills, both written and oral, are also needed; it does little good to discover something important if you can't convey it to your audience. This includes the lay audience. And if fieldwork is your bag, it helps to be in shape!"

Poole's work does in fact involve a certain amount of time in the field studying animals. Early in his career, he spent weeks and sometimes months in the field, collecting data and observing wildlife. He stresses that those interested in fieldwork must be hardy and adaptable, as it can include exposure to very harsh conditions—extreme cold or heat, wet or dry, high altitude, and biting insects. "I once spent a week studying lynx in the Northwest Territories [of Canada] when the overnight temperatures were minus forty-two degrees Celsius and the warmest part of the day was in the low minus thirties," Poole says. "And bugs . . . I can tell you stories about mosquitoes and blackflies!" Another valuable skill, Poole says, is "the ability to fly in small aircraft without getting sick." Among the personality traits helpful for this career, Poole cites "a love of the outdoors and a passion for what you are doing." He notes that wildlife biologists also need to be able to work well with people.

The typical wildlife biologist career path that Poole describes begins with summer and postgraduate work as a wildlife technician, which offers invaluable experience. The next step is designing and conducting research while gaining a master's or a doctorate. Once in the job market, the first step is working at the junior wildlife biologist level. Eventually people work up to more senior positions with greater responsibility. An alternative route is to look for jobs in administration or management, especially if the biologist is not interested in field-work. Poole emphasizes the value of membership in a professional wildlife organization; it helps expand your horizons and further defines the work.

A typical day in the life of a wildlife biologist is hard to describe, Poole says. It depends on the projects he is working on at the moment. One week in late August 2002 was "in the field picking up GPS [global positioning system] radio collars that I remotely removed from moose in British Columbia, and I spent three days in a helicopter in the Rocky Mountains counting mountain goats. I have spent weeks, sometimes months, in the field collecting data and observing wildlife. These days, I seem to spend a great deal of time in front of the computer, designing studies, analyzing data, and writing reports and papers."

Recent technology plays an important role in his work. "Computer skills are essential," says Poole, including GIS (geographic information system) mapping, data management, using email, and being familiar with the Internet. "The Internet means that I can work practically anywhere and still be connected to clients and colleagues." A thorough understanding of statistics is also essential, as is the ability to adapt to changing technologies, such as the recent use of GPS collars on wildlife to record animal locations and aid in population and habitat studies.

Poole believes that his career will always be important and is likely to become even more so as environmental concerns increase. An uncertain factor is the fluctuation in government priorities and funding, and job competition is likely to remain fierce.

His advice to anyone interested in a career in wildlife biology is to volunteer to get some experience and try it out first. "Then," he says, "when you are sure it's what you want to do, build up your education and work on your experience. Good schooling and mentors are important. Meet people who may further your career. My colleague and I get many resumes, but we tend to key in on the people that call or visit."

Another important factor is flexibility about where you live and work. "Not everyone can practice wildlife biology in downtown Toronto," says Poole. "My best career move in life was moving to the Northwest Territories and cutting my professional teeth in an area where wildlife was so important, research was well funded, and competition for jobs was low."

Poole worked for fifteen years for the government in the Northwest Territories. He has worked as a consultant for the past five years. Although he notes some downsides to this work, such as government "red tape" and dealing with difficult supervisors, Poole continues to be enthusiastic about his career as a wildlife biologist. He's happy to point out the rewards of his job. He likes the fact that his work with wild animals can make a difference to their populations, and that he's doing something that matters to wildlife and the environment. And once, while handling gyrfalcons on the Arctic coast, he says with satisfaction, "my assistant noted that we were getting paid to do something tourists would pay thousands to do!"

Profile

WILDLIFE REHABILITATOR
Sharon Kzinowek

"I've had a lifelong passion for nature, especially wildlife," says Sharon Kzinowek, a wildlife rehabilitator at the Wildlife Center of Virginia (WCV) near Waynesboro. "As a child, I played with stuffed animals, not dolls, and although I grew up in Chicago, I was taught a respect for nature and spent many summers camping in Wisconsin."

Kzinowek's definition of her work is simple: "I rehabilitate injured and orphaned wild animals with the intent to release them back into the wild." In the process, "I also teach others how to do this work."

The general public, park rangers, and licensed rehabilitators bring animals to the WCV, which has a full-scale hospital for native wildlife. The facility cares for native species only, however; any non-native animals that turn up are sent to an appropriate care center for exotics. While the animals are being physically rehabilitated, Kzinowek is careful that they have a minimal amount of human contact. Birds, for example, go through a stage called imprinting; if young birds become imprinted on a human, they are nonreleasable. Towels may be hung to reduce visual contact with staff and minimize animal stress and habituation to humans. Handling is kept to a minimum to help ensure that the animal will be able to be released back into the wild. Additionally, baby animals are never raised by themselves: every attempt must be made to find foster siblings for both mammals and birds. Says Kzi-nowek, "A rehabilitator must be willing either to take in another animal of the same species and appropriate age or give up the orphan in their care to another rehabber with the appropriate sibling."

Some animals are nonreleasable because of the extent of their injuries. Most of these animals are kept at the center or transferred to zoos, nature centers, or some other facility that has a permit to keep wild animals for use in education. "It is illegal in most states to keep any nonreleasable wild animal simply as a pet," Kzinowek says. "Factors must be considered about whether a particular animal would be suitable for living out its life in captivity. Some species in general do not do well in a captive setting; individual animals may show signs of too much stress, or their injuries may cause them pain or have other long-term effects." Animals that are nonreleasable and unsuitable candidates for education are humanely euthanized.

Describing a typical workday is difficult for Kzinowek, because the tasks vary from season to season. "Spring and summer are busy, with a hectic schedule of orphan mammal, songbird, and raptor feedings. Typical tasks include preparing meals, providing proper housing and exercise, and observing patients. Additionally, I train volunteers and licensed rehabilitators and give presentations concerning many different aspects of wildlife rehabilitation."

Public education is, in fact, a very important part of Kzinowek's work as a wildlife rehabilitator. Many things that the public does—littering, for example—have a very negative effect on wildlife. She often has to convince people that baby animals should be left alone. (Generally speaking, wild animals do not require our assistance; they do not make good pets and are not better off living in captivity.)

Current technology has changed the way Kzinowek does her job. "Technology helps us document what we do, compiling statistics of animals received," she says, "and helps make record-keeping efficient. This allows us to spend more time dealing directly with the welfare of the animals and to keep thorough records that may help us in the future with another animal." She also makes PowerPoint presentations, and the center is working on a worldwide disease surveillance system.

Kzinowek has no academic studies beyond high school. She came to this work as a volunteer and received her training from the WCV itself. She suggests, however, that college courses in biology or the environmental sciences would be helpful to those interested in this work. And experience working with animals, through volunteering or otherwise, is very important. Kzinowek considers a strong knowledge base of natural history or native wildlife important for her job, as well as animal husbandry skills.

According to Kzinowek, personality traits that are helpful for wildlife rehabilitators are "patience, good communication skills, dedication, and general concern for the natural environment and its inhabitants." She describes the working conditions as "very fast-paced, requiring extreme attention to detail. There is never a dull moment."

Citing a typical career path is difficult, says Kzinowek, because there are few paid jobs in wildlife rehabilitation and no formal training. Her own experience offers one possible career path. "I started out as a volunteer at the center, became licensed by the state, and worked at a veterinary clinic. Then I was offered a full-time, paid position at WCV."

"Most wildlife rehabilitators are volunteers, with all expenses coming out of their own pockets," says Kzinowek. She therefore doesn't see this work as having a great deal of financial promise. Competition for the few paying jobs is quite intense. She advises persons interested in becoming a rehabilitator to volunteer to help a local rehabilitator or center in their area.

Kzinowek can easily list the things about her work that she doesn't like: "I dislike the frustrations over the general ignorance of the public when it comes to wildlife and the environment. I also dislike when an animal that I have worked hard to save does not make it." The compensation for Kzinowek is that she has a much longer list of things that she likes about her work. "I like being part of the solution to help the wild creatures that humans have such an adverse effect on, and the close contact with wild animals. I also enjoy the fast pace, constant change, learning something new every day, and insight into the wild kingdom." Contact with the public is another good part of her work. "I enjoy teaching the general public what they can do to minimize the impact humans have on wild animals."

But Kzinowek is most impassioned about the work with the animals themselves: "Giving an animal a second chance in its natural environment is the best part of my job."

Chapter 8

Ranch Animals

Ranching never has been a great living, but it sure is a great life.

Elmer Kelton

Western novelist Elmer Kelton viewed living and working on a full-time ranch as more of a lifestyle issue than a career. For many people, it's a very satisfying lifestyle; some even say that the benefits go beyond developing top-quality animals to rewards that can't be measured quantitatively. They emphasize the total involvement of the family, teaching children about farming, and work that is not run by the clock.

This chapter uses terminology from the United States Department of Agriculture (USDA). For most departmental statistics and information, the USDA uses the term "farm" for a unit of land that grows crops; "ranch" indicates a unit of land used for raising livestock, even though to many people a ranch is a very large area of land instead of a reference to how that land is used.

Some ranchers choose to live on a hobby ranch, where they have a little acreage and can dabble in raising animals, but do not derive their primary income from these pursuits. This gives them some of the pleasures of ranching but not total financial dependence on it. Many people breed and raise animals because they grew up doing so and it's a life they know. Some ranchers grew up in cities, however, and are attracted to this work nonetheless.

People interested in ranching but who have not grown up on a ranch should realize that raising animals is much more complicated than the casual observer might at first suspect. Many different issues must be considered when planning a ranch. People with no experience in the field who want to raise animals full-time would be wise to first work for a number of years on someone else's ranch. This will help them decide whether they really want to commit the resources for the necessary land and equipment. In the process, they may also discover they are allergic to certain animals, feeds, or bedding material.

This chapter gives a general introduction to most kinds of animals raised on ranches, with brief mention of some of the issues involved in raising them. These animals include beef and dairy cattle, pigs, sheep, goats, poultry, and a variety of other less traditional animals such as ratites (flightless birds such as emus), llamas and alpacas, deer and elk, wild boars, and American bison (commonly known as buffalo). Many of these are raised in a setting that includes other animals. Anyone interested in ranching should investigate in further detail all the specifics about raising a particular type of animal. Universities or colleges with agriculture programs have information and animal facilities that you can visit. Government departments and farmers' organizations also have helpful information. Talking to people who raise the animal of interest at agricultural fairs can provide yet more data about this work.

SOME RANCHING CONCERNS

Like farmers who till the soil and raise crops, people who raise animals must deal with many factors that are beyond their control. Ranchers who graze their animals on pasture face periodic droughts and the resulting cost of buying grain and hay. Diseases, some unforeseen and quick-spreading, can have a bad or even catastrophic effect on the market for specific animals. After bovine spongiform encephalopathy (commonly known as mad cow disease) was found in Canada in 2003, a headline in the *Ottawa Citizen* read: "Cows sell for less than a bale of hay."

Many environmental issues arise when animals are bred and raised on a large scale. Concerns about animal waste are among the most serious. Other issues relate to the use of medications in raising animals. Concerns have been raised about the discovery of traces of these medications both in the meat and in the environment.

RANCH SIZES

In the United States and Canada, smaller ranches are found in the eastern parts of each country, while larger ranches are in the west. Statistics from the USDA show that the states with the largest ranches are

Arizona, with an average of 2,583 acres per ranch; South Dakota, with 1,377; and North Dakota, with 1,292. In general, these states are dry, so the ranches need to encompass more land. In more temperate climates with more reliable water sources, the ranches can be smaller.

Still, the generally accepted maxim of ranching is that bigger is better. News reports and newspaper articles often present poignant accounts of the demise of small ranches. Many people are able to earn a substantial income on smaller acreages, however. It often involves what is called sustainable farming, which use methods of raising animals and growing crops that are environmentally sound and enhance the land. Smaller "sustainable" ranchers often incorporate more than one moneymaking endeavor into their ranches, so that if one of these is not profitable in one year, the whole enterprise does not sink. This practice stands in sharp contrast to the large enterprises, sometimes known as factory farms, where the entire profitability depends on one type of animal.

CATTLE

Cattle in North America are believed to be a legacy of the second voyage of Columbus, in 1493. Some also were brought to early settlements in Virginia, New England, and New York. By the 1890s, the large herds of wild buffalo had disappeared from the plains. This opened a new range for raising cattle.

Two types of cattle are raised on ranches. Beef cattle are grown to produce high-quality meat; they are well-muscled with powerfully built legs. Dairy animals are designed to produce milk; they are usually leaner and have larger udders than do beef cattle.

Beef

The beef industry is very important in the United States and Canada. The value of the U.S. beef industry in 2003 was estimated at $70 billion. The cattle inventory on January 1, 2003, in the United States was 96.1 million (down from 103.5 million in 1996, when the industry reached its peak) and in Canada was 13.4 million.

As the science and technology of breeding have developed, cattle breeding has become an exacting science no longer dominated by a few individuals who had a knack for breeding cattle. The beef market generally goes through a ten- or twelve-year cycle; eight or so years show growth, followed by several years of decline before the market rebounds and begins to grow again.

A major concern of beef breeders well into the twenty-first century will be efficiency of production because of the competition from other protein sources and a change in eating styles. This concern will provide an incentive for the beef industry to use state-of-the-art breeding technology and the emerging biotechnologies to maximize the profit in producing beef.

For cattle fed organically, traits such as resistance to disease and the ability to eat forage are valued. And for organic production systems, breeds that are less common or crossbreeds may be more important. The USDA's certified organic label indicates that beef cattle have been fed a strictly vegetarian diet. Though organic beef is not yet a large market, it is becoming much more attractive in the face of concerns such as mad cow disease.

Some of the qualities for which beef are bred include what are called "carcass traits"—marbling, rib eye, and back fat—and these can be measured by ultrasound systems. Beef producers also look for cows that calve easily, show good mothering ability, and have a good personality that makes them easy to work with. Some studies indicate that calm cattle gain weight faster and provide more tender meat than ill-tempered cattle. Additionally, animals with poor dispositions can cause damage to equipment and harm handlers.

Dairy

Dairy cows produce milk for human consumption. Dairy cattle breeding has changed recently with the use of artificial insemination, statistical techniques that help estimate the genetic merit of livestock, and improved systems for recording milk production. These tools allow breeders to be far more effective than they have been in the past. The main goal in breeding dairy cows is to raise cows that produce higher yields of desirable-quality milk. Yields per cow have increased dramatically over the last twenty years.

Breeders have also worked to improve other traits in addition to milk production; breeding goals recently have come to include traits associated with longevity, health, and fitness as a way of reducing production costs and improving cow welfare.

The general prediction is for larger and fewer dairy farms in the future. Increased technological advancements in computers and automated equipment will assist in gathering data, and research results can be applied more quickly. As consumer concerns about food safety and animal welfare increase, the health and well-being of cattle and also genetic diversity will become more important. Producers will look for trouble-free cattle that require little individual attention.

Veal

Veal is the meat from a male dairy calf or a young beef animal. To continue producing milk, dairy cows must give birth. Only a few male dairy calves are raised to maturity for use in breeding; otherwise, they are of little value to the dairy farmer.

Veal farmers purchase seven- to ten-day-old calves and raise them to the desired age, usually six or seven months. Many calves are weaned from milk and fed a grain-based diet, although some continue on a milk-based diet. The desired size for milk-fed veal is about five hundred pounds and for grain-fed veal about seven hundred pounds. Calves generally are housed in small pens designed to reduce individual stress but give adequate space. Veal meat is especially valued in many international cuisines.

PIGS

Throughout the world, pork accounts for about fifty percent of the daily meat protein intake. The pork industry is growing rapidly in North America today, with pork being the fourth-largest agricultural sector of all U.S. farm commodities. Pork exports to meet worldwide demand are high, and the retail pork market is thriving.

The pork industry contributes strongly to the U.S. economy, supporting about eight hundred thousand jobs. Modern technology is making pork production more efficient, and it has been moving into regions other than the traditional Corn Belt states, such as Texas, Colorado, and North Carolina.

Canada produces more than seventeen million hogs a year, and about thirty-five percent of this pork is exported. These exports bring in more than $1 billion annually in foreign revenues.

SHEEP

Sheep were domesticated by humans thousands of years ago. Then as today, sheep and lambs were raised for their wool, hides, meat, and milk. Because sheep provide so many different products and can graze on rough terrain, they are popular worldwide. Lambs are prized for the taste of the meat; lamb is a favorite dish in many countries. Sheep's milk has only a small market in the United States, but it is much more popular in other countries. It is high in fat and protein and is used mainly for making cheese. In fact, in total around the world, sheep produce as much milk as do dairy cattle.

On sheep ranches in the United States and Canada, the sheep live in barns, barnyards, or pastures. In areas of the U.S. West, where public rangelands or mountainous areas are used for sheep grazing, shepherds stay outside with the flocks during the grazing season. The use of public lands for sheep grazing is becoming increasingly rare, however, and most sheep are now kept in more restricted areas.

Sheep are often raised on smaller ranches than are cattle, although huge sheep ranches do exist in the western United States and Canada. On the smaller ranches, the owners often care for the sheep themselves, but they sometimes hire extra help during extremely busy seasons, such as lambing or shearing. Sheep are sheared once a year. Larger spreads may hire shearers; they are usually people from countries with a high sheep population who already have much experience working with sheep.

In Canada, most sheep are raised in Ontario, with Alberta the second-largest producer. Sheep numbers have been increasing steadily since 1995, but the number of ranches is dropping. The average flock size on Ontario ranches is approximately sixty-six animals; the largest ranches have five hundred to a thousand animals. Although Canada does export lamb meat, it imports more lambs than it exports. There the focus is on raising lambs for meat and sheep for wool and cheese. The wool market is currently in decline, however.

GOATS

Goats are a versatile species of livestock. Various breeds are raised for their milk, meat, and fibers used in clothing, such as mohair and cashmere. Goat milk and cheese are becoming more popular, especially among individuals with allergies to dairy products. Goat meat is a staple of many different ethnic foods and is especially popular during holiday seasons. Goats are raised worldwide because they can be successfully maintained on marginal or even rough terrain.

POULTRY

Chickens and turkeys are raised for meat and egg production; a very few are raised to show. Generally, the birds raised for meat are kept in specially designed, temperature-controlled buildings to minimize predator problems and provide a healthy environment. Birds raised for egg production are kept in buildings that have special nesting boxes.

Some producers sell free-range organic chickens, which live outside, eat natural diets, and are free of antibiotics. Many people consider this meat better-tasting than that of chickens raised in a more controlled environment. It also has a higher nutritional value.

OTHER RANCH ANIMALS

Many other, less traditional animals are raised. Emus, part of the ratite family of flightless birds, is one such animal that was initially considered to have great promise. Emu meat is low in fat and cholesterol, is higher in protein than chicken and in vitamin E and iron than beef, and is said to taste like filet mignon. Emu oil is used in many products. The feathers could be used in fashion designs, and the skin leather for other products. Even with these desirable attributes, the market for emu products is not large, although a good number of emus are still being raised.

Llamas and alpacas have been domesticated in South America for centuries. There, llamas are used as beasts of burden and a meat source, and their wool is used as a fiber in making clothing. Alpacas are raised primarily for their wool, which is soft, fine, warm, and strong, although South Americans also eat alpaca meat. In North America, llamas and alpacas are often part of a diversified farming operation; their ability to exist on marginal pastureland makes them valuable. Income from these animals here comes from their wool and live sales for breeding stock. Llamas, which are easily trained, are also used to pull carts, as companion pets, and as guardians for sheep or goats.

Other animals, some usually classified as wild animals, are also raised for their meat. These include domestic ducks and geese; deer and elk, wild boars, and bison are often raised for on-ranch hunting, although raising them for meat is expected to increase.

For information on raising these nontraditional animals, contact your local government agricultural department and talk to breeders who raise them. Additional information can be found on the Internet and in libraries. Because the government regulates some of these animals, checking whether there are any regulations concerning the animals of interest is an essential first step.

See profile on page 42.

RESOURCES

Alpaca Owners and Breeders Association (AOBA)
17000 Commerce Parkway, Suite C
Mt. Laurel, NJ 08054
phone: 800-213-9522
fax: 856-439-0525
email: aoba@ahint.com
www.alpacainfo.com

American Beef Journal
130 Oakland Road
Maynardville, TN 37807
phone: 800-727-1904
fax: 423-447-6452
www.theamericanbeefjournal.com

American Dairy Goat Association
209 West Main Street, P.O. Box 865
Spindale, NC 28160
phone: 828-286-3801
fax: 828-287-0476
email: info@adga.org
www.adga.org

American Emu Association
P.O. Box 224
Sixes, OR 97476
phone: 541-332-0675
fax: 928-962-9430
email: info@aea-emu.org
www.aea-emu.org

American National CattleWomen (ANCW)
P.O. Box 3881
Englewood, CO 80155
phone: 303-694-0313
fax: 303-694-2390
email: ancw@beef.org
www.ancw.org

American Pastured Poultry Producers Association
P.O. Box 1024
Chippewa Falls, WI 54729
phone: 715-667-5501
fax: 715-667-3044
email: grit@appa.org
www.apppa.org

Canadian Federation of Agriculture (CFA)
75 Albert Street, Suite 1101
Ottawa, Ontario
Canada K1P 5E7
phone: 613-236-3633
fax: 613-236-5749
www.cfa-fca.ca

Chicken Farmers of Canada
1007-350 Sparks St.
Ottawa, Ontario
Canada K1N 7S8
phone: 613-241-2800
fax: 613-241-5999
email: cfc@chicken.ca
www.chicken.ca

Humane Farming Association
P.O. Box 3577
San Rafael, CA 94912
phone: 415-771-2253
fax: 415-485-0106
email: hfa@hfa.org
www.hfa.org

Llama Association of North America (LANA)
1800 South Obenchain Road
Eagle Point, OR 97524
phone: 541-830-5161
email: llamainfo@aol.com
www.llamainfo.org

Livestock Plus
P.O. Box 391
Clarion, IA 50525
www.livestockplus.net

National Cattlemen's Beef Association
9110 East Nichols Avenue, Suite 300
Centennial, CO 80112
phone: 303-694-0305
fax: 303-694-2851
www.beefusa.org

National Pork Producers Council
10664 Justin Drive
Urbandale, IA 50322
phone: 515-278-8012
fax: 515-278-8011
www.nppc.org

North American Deer Farmers Association
1720 West Wisconsin Avenue
Appleton, WI 54914-3254
phone: 920-734-0934
fax: 920-734-0955
email: info@nadefa.org
www.nadefa.org

North American Elk Breeders Association
P.O. Box 1640
Platte City, MO 64079
phone: 816-431-3605
fax: 816-431-2705
email: info@naelk.org
www.naelk.org

Ontario Farm Animal Council
7195 Millcreek Drive
Mississauga, Ontario
Canada L5N 4H1
fax: 905-858-1589
email: ofac@idirect.com
www.ofac.org

Ontario Sheep Marketing Agency
130 Malcolm Road
Guelph, Ontario
Canada N1K 1B1
phone: 519-836-0043
fax: 519-836-2531
email: general@ontariosheep.org
www.ontariosheep.org

United States Poultry and Egg Association
1530 Cooledge Road
Tucker, GA 30084-7303
phone: 770-493-9401
fax: 770-493-9257
www.poultryegg.org

Websites

Centralized information on the dairy industy, including jobs, which can be accessed by members at www.dairynetwork.com.

People wishing to provide sanctuaries for farm animals can use www.farmanimalshelters.org as a resource.

Chapter 9

Exotic Animals

The greater cats with golden eyes
Stare out between the bars.
Deserts are there, and different skies,
At night with different stars.
     Vita Sackville-West, *The King's Daughter*

Exotic animals such as lions, tigers, elephants, and other non-native creatures attract many people. To see these animals in North America, people go to zoos, private animal parks, and sanctuaries. These are also the places to go to find work with exotic animals.

A wide variety of jobs can be found in these settings. Job requirements are just as varied. Some zoo jobs involve working directly with the animals; others may be in support or management positions. Sanctuaries, because they are usually much smaller in size and scope than zoos, have less-specialized types of work available. Private parks may focus on only one or a few kinds of animals. The work in these settings is quite similar to zoo or sanctuary work.

ZOOS

Historians generally agree that Pharaoh Hatshepsut founded the first known zoo in Egypt around the year 1500 B.C. Some five hundred years later, emperor Wen Wang founded an enormous zoo known as the Garden of Intelligence in China. Still later, zoos were used for educating Greek students. During the age of exploration, Europeans housed the unusual creatures brought back from distant lands in zoos.

Today zoos usually focus on educating people about the natural world. They work to promote public awareness of and involvement in the conservation of species. Some zoos also conduct research into wildlife management.

Many zoos have breeding programs designed to conserve and propagate species that are threatened in the wild. These captive breeding programs, still in their infancy, are not always successful, particularly with giant pandas, elephants, killer whales, cheetahs, hummingbirds, and reptiles. Problems with inbreeding of a species are partially solved with the use of embryo transfer, artificial insemination, and database lists of available breeding stock. Because of the limited success of captive breeding, many environmentalists emphasize the need to save habitats as the best means to prevent extinction. But these two solutions to the extinction of animal species—captive breeding and habitat preservation—both present many challenges.

The physical setup of the earliest zoos is not known, but until fairly recently, most zoos housed their animals in cages that were not necessarily spacious. In the 1950s and '60s, some zoos began to change in an attempt to re-create, as much as possible, natural habitats for the animals they housed. These zoos often used more natural means—moats, ravines, and so on—to define the habitat for the animals, and they tried to obscure any man-made construction elements.

Zoos today generally organize their animal exhibits in one of three different ways. One type centers on the habitat and ecosystems in which the animals live. These settings include a variety of species and show the interdependency among the animals, habitat, and ecosystem. There are ten basic categories of habitats and ecosystems: desert; island; ocean and coastline; prairie and steppe; river, lake, and wetland; savanna; scrubland; temperate forest and taiga; tropical rain forest; and tundra. The second major method of organization is by animal categories: amphibians, birds, mammals, reptiles, and insects. Some zoos use a third method of organization, using zoogeographical location to group the animals. In this method, the animals are organized by geography according to similar places of origin, rather than by species or habitat. Categories may include Africa, Asia, Australia, Central America and the Caribbean, Europe, North America, the Pacific Islands, South America, or appropriate combinations thereof. Zoos may also integrate their displays so that some are by animal types, others by habitats and ecosystems, and some by location.

The work available at zoos varies widely. In some ways a zoo can be compared to a small city, and many of the jobs at a zoo are similar to the work needed to keep a city functioning. Zoo work offers three different levels of involvement with the animals: positions that involve direct work with the animals, jobs that require knowledge about animals but not direct work with the animals, and administrative work that is necessary to keep the institution functioning but requires no knowledge of or work with the animals. Although every job varies from zoo to zoo, the list that follows gives an idea of the types of positions in these three categories. The names given to jobs in these positions vary among zoos and often among countries, so when checking job ads, read the job descriptions carefully.

Direct Work with Animals

General curator. Oversees the entire animal collection and animal management staff; plans strategic collection.

Animal curator. Manages either a section or all of the animal collection.

Conservation biologist/zoologist. Provides scientific and technical assistance in managing the animals and assists with research or field conservation.

Exhibit curator. Creates exhibits and assists in graphic design.

Head keeper/aquarist. Supervises a section or department of the institution; provides training and scheduling for keepers.

Keeper/aquarist. Provides daily care for animals, including preparing food and cleaning; maintains exhibits; keeps records.

Registrar. Maintains records on the animal collection and applies for permits and licenses as needed for holding or transporting animals.

Senior keeper/aquarist. Provides primary animal care in one department.

Veterinarian. Oversees animal health care and record maintenance.

Veterinary technician. Assists the veterinarian, caring for the animals under veterinary supervision.

Docent/volunteer. May work with small animals, prepare diets, lead tours, teach in educational programs, and staff special events.

Knowledge about Animals

Zoo director. Carries out policies as directed by the governing authority, plans for future development, and oversees the institution's operation.

Assistant director. Assists the director, taking charge in his or her absence.

Curator/coordinator/director of research. Supervises research, acts as liaison with academic community, and writes for scientific journals.

Curator/coordinator/director of conservation. Oversees the institution's conservation activities; acts as liaison with government wildlife agencies and other conservation organizations.

Education curator. Plans and carries out educational programs.

Horticulture curator. Oversees the botanical collection and its use for the animals; provides daily grounds maintenance.

Marketing director/manager. Creates advertising and plans activities to increase public knowledge of the institution.

Public relations/affairs manager/director. Uses the media to promote the institution and its mission and programs.

Special events manager/coordinator. Plans and coordinates events to attract visitors.

Volunteer coordinator. Recruits volunteers or docents and schedules their activities; informs them of new developments to communicate to the public.

Administrative Work

Development director/officer. Develops and manages fund-raising, including writing grant proposals, attracting sponsors, and soliciting donations.

Finance manager/director. Manages finances, including paying bills, purchasing, investing, and preparing financial statements.

Gift shop manager. Manages gift shop staff and all aspects of the gift shop from product purchase to shop design.

Membership director/manager. Maintains and increases individual and family memberships, designing special events for members.

Operations director/manager. Oversees daily operation of the physical plant and equipment.

Personnel manager/director. Oversees all personnel matters, including payroll, insurance, and taxes.

Visitor services manager. Supervises the staff and facilities used by the visiting public, including concessions and restrooms.

An overriding requirement for all of these positions is a commitment to animal welfare and the conservation of species. Zoo jobs may also involve extra time, as animals sometimes may require around-the-clock attention. Many of the positions in zoos are popular, and competition can be strong. Volunteer work in zoos is very important to the institution's operation, as funding often is not secure, and volunteers supplement work done by staff. Many zoos have quite extensive volunteer programs. These can be invaluable to those interested in zoo work; they offer a way to learn about the work before beginning studies, spend time with animals while working full-time at another job, and gain experience helpful in obtaining a full-time zoo job.

The background and qualifications needed for each of the listed jobs are very different. Jobs that entail working closely with the animals on a daily basis may require advanced degrees, as in veterinary work, or they may require some kind training, as in veterinary technician or zookeeper jobs.

To give an idea of the number of jobs that can be found in a large metropolitan-area zoo, the Toronto Zoo website in 2004 listed slightly more than 250 full-time positions. Of these, 133 were in the areas of biology and conservation, which included all of the jobs involving direct work with the animals plus a few in research and administration. The animal population of the Toronto Zoo at that time—more than 5,000—represented slightly more than 450 different species. The Toronto Zoo covers 710 acres and is organized into five zoogeographic regions: IndoMalaya, Africa, the Americas (North and South), Eurasia, and Australasia. Many of the types of work available in zoos are covered elsewhere in this book. For information on veterinarian and veterinary technician positions, see pages 178 and 180. For information on aviculture, the care of birds kept in captivity, and bird training, see pages 81 and 84. For a zookeeper profile, see page 126. For information on aquarist and marine mammal trainer positions, see Chapter 5. For an aquarist profile, see page 108.

Two typical positions in zoos or animal parks—curator and keeper—are described below. The profiles at the end of the chapter look at the work of an elephant handler and the owners of a sanctuary for exotic animals.

CURATOR

Salary Range: Varies, but generally from $19,000 to $66,050.

Educational Requirements: A degree in life sciences or zoology—at least a master's degree, although a doctorate may be preferred.

Employment Outlook: Expected to increase in the near term, as zoo attendance has been increasing, but jobs are very competitive.

A zoo curator (sometimes called animal curator) oversees research programs and manages the zoo's collection of animals. The curator may be responsible for all of the animals in the zoo or for only a part of the collection.

Curators develop long-range plans for the animal collection in a zoo or animal park. They decide which species to acquire for a collection and which species or animals to send to other zoos. They select and manage conservation and breeding programs, often working closely with other wildlife organizations and agencies. Such programs usually involve species that are endangered in the wild, so this work may involve worldwide travel to study these species in their natural habitat and meet with animal experts in other parts of the world. A curator's work with captive-animal breeding programs presents a number of challenges. Curators must stay in contact with other zoo breeding programs to gain information and share knowledge to meet these challenges.

Curators oversee the daily care and feeding of animals and the work of the keeper staff. They also write and manage the policies for the care of animals. Curators help design exhibits for the animals, which must be comfortable and realistic settings. Curators also may be involved in developing a zoo's education program.

In their management role, curators oversee the keeper staff, hiring and training personnel as necessary, and develop and manage the zoo's budget. Curators must work well as supervisors and team members. Verbal and written communication skills are important for curators; they must be able to work well with staff, communicate with external experts, and write reports. They also must work well with professionals around the world. Compliance with laws regarding wildlife collection, trade, and transportation is the responsibility of the curator. Curators act as liaisons between their zoos and government agencies that regulate wildlife. Besides zoos, curators work in aquariums and safari or wild animal parks, but the pay in such settings is usually less than at zoos.

For more information on curators, see aviculture on page 81.

KEEPER

Salary Range: Averages between $6 and $14 an hour.

Educational Requirements: On-the-job training is most common; some keeper positions require a bachelor's degree.

Employment Outlook: The outlook is not good. Zoo capacity is growing slowly, job turnover is low, and the competition for available positions is keen.

Zookeepers, often called simply keepers or animal care workers, work directly with the animals. They prepare the food and feed the animals every day, assist with the care of sick or injured animals, and may help raise very young animals. Depending upon the size and organization of the zoo, keepers may work with a broad group of animals, such as birds, reptiles, or mammals, or they may work with only particular kinds of animals, such as large cats, primates, or small mammals.

Zookeepers need to understand the behavior of animals and wildlife and know how to care for animals. They must be well organized and careful as they complete the daily records on animal conditions and food intake, and they need to be observant. Because they see the animals every day, they must be aware of changes in behavior or eating patterns or direct signs of illness or injury that should be recorded and reported to medical staff. Good communication skills also are important for zookeepers. They often interact with the visiting public by giving presentations or leading group tours, which usually include answering questions.

Zookeepers must be in good physical condition. Much of what they do on a daily basis is hard work. They lift cages, carriers, heavy bags of feed, and bales of hay. They may need to lift, hold, or restrain animals, risking getting bitten or scratched. They may kneel, crawl, or bend repeatedly. They clean the enclosures and are especially concerned with removing litter that may be harmful to animals.

Keepers may work outdoors in all types of weather—heat, cold, rain, sleet, or snow. Their hours are irregular. Because animals need to be fed every day, keepers often must work on weekends and holidays.

Zookeepers need to have a deep love of animals and gain satisfaction from working with them. Their work may be physically and emotionally draining and, at times, even dangerous. Despite these drawbacks, the competition for zookeeping jobs is intense. Individuals who have work experience with animals, particularly in a zoo or animal-park setting, will have an edge in obtaining keeper jobs.

See profiles on pages 126 and 169.

SANCTUARY WORK

Animal sanctuaries are places of refuge for injured, abused, abandoned, neglected, displaced, and unwanted animals. They cater to both exotic and domestic animals. The only alternative for these animals would be suffering, living in an unsuitable location, or death. Sanctuaries provide lifetime care or, when possible, adoption to carefully screened homes, in the case of farm or companion animals. Some sanctuaries try to rehabilitate and return wild animals to the wild.

Animals come to sanctuaries from different sources. Many are surplus stock from zoos or research institutions. Others are the results of misguided attempts to make abandoned wild baby animals into pets. Sanctuaries may also have domestic animals that were rescued from slaughter and companion animals that were homeless or abandoned. In short, all of the animals found in sanctuaries have been displaced from their normal niches in nature or human homes and usually cannot return to these places.

Sanctuaries recognize the value of all life and the obligation that many feel to correct the wrongs done to animals. Among the goals of sanctuaries are to educate humans and change the way that they often treat animals. An essential aspect of sanctuaries is that the well-being of the residents—the animals under care—comes first. Sanctuary workers believe that all creatures in the sanctuary are of equal importance.

Operating or working in an animal sanctuary can be very rewarding but also very draining. The work involves a great deal of time spent caring for the animals and sometimes runs up against opposition from sanctuary neighbors, who may not wish to have numbers of captive wild or domestic animals nearby.

Sanctuaries are virtually always smaller—in both space and numbers of animals—than the average-size zoo, and the work is much less specialized. Almost all sanctuaries operate on a shoestring budget; in fact, the owner or head of a sanctuary often receives a salary from some other line of work. Most sanctuaries are dependent on contributions, financial and otherwise, from individuals who care about the mission of the sanctuary; most use volunteers for much of the work they do. Each sanctuary is set up differently, so contacting a specific sanctuary is the best way to learn of possible volunteer or work positions.

Sanctuaries exist for virtually all types of animals and birds. A quick search on the Internet will locate sanctuaries around the world.

See profile on page 171.

RESOURCES

American Zoo and Aquarium Association
8403 Colesville Road, Suite 710
Silver Spring, MD 20910-3314
phone: 301-562-0777
fax: 301-562-0888
email: generalinquiry@aza.org
www.aza.org

Animal Protection Institute (API)
P.O. Box 22505
Sacramento, CA 95822
phone: 916-447-3085
fax: 916-447-3070
email: info@api4animals.org
www.api4animals.org

The Association of Sanctuaries (TAOS)
1013 Lesa Lane
Garland, TX 75042
phone: 972-485-5647
fax: 972-487-9843
email: taos5@aol.com
www.taosanctuaries.org

Canadian Association of Zoos and Aquariums (CAZA)
www.caza.ca

Canadian Coalition for Farm Animals (CCFA)
213–33 Hazleton Avenue
Toronto, Ontario
Canada M5R 2E3
phone: 866-303-2232
fax: 604-266-9749
email: info@humanefood.ca
www.humanefood.ca

Defenders of Wildlife National Headquarters
1130 17th Street, NW
Washington, DC 20036
phone: 202-682-9400
email: info@defenders.org
www.defenders.org

Elephant Managers Association
1 Conservation Place
Syracuse, NY 13204
email: emaboard@elephant-managers.com
www.elephant-managers.com

Fauna Foundation
P.O. Box 33
Chambly, Quebec
Canada J3L 4B1
phone: 450-658-1844
fax: 450-658-2202
email: fauna.found@sympatico.ca
www.faunafoundation.org

Moorpark College
Exotic Animal Training and Management Program
7075 Campus Road
Moorpark, CA 93021
phone: 805-378-1400
email: eatm@vcccd.net
www.sunny.moorparkcollege.edu

Smithsonian National Zoological Park
3001 Connecticut Avenue, NW
Washington, DC 20008
phone: 202-673-0209
www.natzoo.si.edu

Websites
The Zoological Society of San Diego website includes numerous job profiles. Use the search engine at www.sandiegozoo.org.

Profile

SENIOR ELEPHANT HANDLER
April Yoder

"The best part of my job is that I get to work around elephants," says April Yoder, senior elephant handler (or elephant manager) at Oregon's Zoo in Portland. "A friend of mine summed it up when he said, 'It is a privilege to work with elephants.'"

Yoder develops the zoo's entire elephant program, which includes coordinating, developing, and implementing educational programs; providing ideas and information to her supervisors; and scheduling and overseeing daily operations of the barn and staff. "As senior keeper," she says, "I am basically responsible for every aspect of the elephants' well-being. This includes physical care: diet and nutrition, foot care, skin care, coordinating veterinary procedures, and so forth. It also includes their mental health. Elephants are very intelligent and need to be mentally stimulated through behavior enrichment and training." Elephants receive daily training on new behaviors; some of these behaviors help with veterinary procedures, and others provide exercise and stimulation for the elephants.

Although Yoder rarely has a typical day, she does certain things every day. Each day begins with a morning meeting, where the elephant staff discusses the plans for the day and current issues, such as upcoming veterinary procedures, maintenance, and tours.

Cleaning is a major part of her work with elephants. Manure must be picked up every day and leftover hay raked from all the yards. The rooms where the elephants stay at night are cleaned, hosed, disinfected, and hosed again. Elephant cows are bathed almost every day and the bulls at least once a week. This means hosing off the animals and removing any fecal stains. "It is quite a job to scrub a ten-foot six-inch bull elephant that weighs thirteen thousand pounds," Yoder says.

Footwork is a regular concern. "The nails and pad on the bottom of an elephant's foot grow continuously," Yoder explains. "Since elephants do not walk as much in captivity as they do in the wild, they can get overgrown. Therefore, we have to trim the nails and the pads." It takes about an hour to trim one foot, and trimming must take place at least once a month.

According to Yoder, a prerequisite for her position is a degree in the life sciences. Because the elephant field is so competitive, she suggests that people interested in this work volunteer at a facility to gain experience, get a feel for the job, meet elephant professionals, and determine whether they really want to do this type of work.

Yoder began her first job with elephants about fourteen years ago. After obtaining a bachelor of science degree in biology, she took a seasonal job with a variety of animals at Paramount's Kings Dominion near Richmond, Virginia. When a position working with elephants became open, Yoder jumped at the chance. At Kings Dominion, Yoder moved from senior handler to zoology operations supervisor.

When Kings Dominion closed, Yoder became a swing keeper, filling in for keepers on their days off, at the Audubon Zoo in New Orleans. This included some work with elephants, and she usually went to the elephant barn after she finished her other work. She eventually became senior elephant keeper at the Audubon Zoo. After a few years, Yoder had an "early midlife crisis" in which she questioned whether she could physically work with elephants for the rest of her life and whether she wanted to continue to earn such a low salary.

Shortly afterward, she moved to the Phoenix Zoo in Arizona to become lead keeper. Her responsibilities there were the daily operations of the Tropics Trail, which included elephants as well as orangutans, ocelots, otter, clouded leopards, spectacled bears, howler and spider monkeys, and lemurs. Her involvement with the elephant program was limited and not on a daily basis. Two management promotions later found Yoder spending about ninety percent of her time behind a desk. She didn't really enjoy the management aspect of the work, and she missed contact with the animals, especially the elephants. So she moved to her current position at the Oregon Zoo. "I can honestly say that this time I will not leave elephants again," she says. "I enjoy having the responsibility of a senior keeper, and I spend eighty-five percent of my time with the elephants."

Although she loves her career, Yoder says it is very physical, mentally taxing, and not a nine-to-five job. "I can guarantee you will get dirty," she says. She loves working outside most of the time and "not being stuck in an office at a desk all day," but she often faces the challenge of working in temperatures that can range from below zero to 118 F. Yoder says that the worst thing about this career is that elephant handlers don't make very much money. Those who do are in upper zoo management, not on the front line. "I always tell people who are interested in this field to do it because they love it and not for the money." She also notes that they have to be willing to move. "You definitely don't find elephant jobs on every corner." Qualities necessary to work with elephants, says Yoder, include patience, being a team player, good observation skills, and a good work ethic.

Knowledge of elephant behavior and good training skills are essential for personal safety. "There is no doubt that this is a dangerous profession simply because of the sheer size of the animals," says Yoder. "You must learn each individual elephant's behavioral patterns and know when something is different. There are also policies in place to help prevent accidents and injuries. For example, we have the two-person rule, which states that there must be two qualified elephant handlers present while working the elephants."

On the job, Yoder uses modern technology extensively. The computer has helped her communicate with elephant people all over the world, and she finds getting and sharing information much easier. "You would be surprised how small the elephant community has become as a result of modern technology," she says. "Most of my communication is done via email. There are even bulletin boards and listserves where elephant people can discuss ideas."

Yoder believes that the outlook for this career is good. "As long as we have elephants in captivity, we will need qualified people to take care of them," she says. It will almost certainly continue to be a competitive field, however.

Profile

ANIMAL SANCTUARY OWNERS
Joe and Pat Bergeron

"Everything revolves around the animals," says Joe Bergeron, co-owner with wife Pat of Bergeron's Exotic Animal Sanctuary near Picton, Ontario. "We are directly involved with the lives of all the animals." When they talk about their work, both Joe and Pat are emphatic: work at the sanctuary is a lifestyle, not a job. They work seven days a week, often more than eight hours a day, but this does not bother them. "Even though it's a lot of work, and even after more than fifteen years, it's a pleasure and a privilege to work around the animals," Joe says.

It is a lifestyle that they didn't anticipate having when they accepted their first big cat in 1987. At the time, Joe was an animal control officer for the town of Picton and also worked with the local

Humane Society. When the Bergerons acquired Casey the cougar, says Pat, "our eyes were opened to the fact that exotic animals also needed places of refuge. There are no Humane Societies for exotics."

Other animals soon followed. Axel, a male cougar, came the next year as a companion for Casey. "At first we had no plan to own many animals," says Joe, "but over time we were offered more." Today the sanctuary has about 150 animals, representing more than thirty-five different species.

The Bergerons have always loved animals. When they moved from the city in 1984 to raise their kids in a rural area, it was, says Joe, "like moving to another planet." The large number of stray, unwanted cats and dogs that roamed the area bothered them. A few years after their move, Joe asked the town of Picton if something could be done about these strays, and shortly afterward he was offered the job of animal control officer. At the time, the Bergerons were breeding German shepherds and running a boarding kennel. But it was difficult to find good homes for the dogs they bred, so the sanctuary is now their main focus.

Originally the Bergerons took surplus zoo animals; now they take animals that have problems or former pets that, for various reasons, can no longer be cared for by their original owners. With their animal collection growing, Pat and Joe applied to the township in 1993 for a permit to open to the public. In addition to the educational value of seeing these rescued animals, they realized that revenue from admission fees would help pay for the care and feeding of the animals.

Joe and Pat divide the duties of feeding the animals between the two of them. Pat feeds the smaller animals—servals (African wildcats), primates, farm animals, baby animals, and birds. She also cares for the house animals—five housecats, five exotic cats, and two dogs. Joe takes care of the big animals—lions, tigers, and wolves. Their normal feeding routines take Pat and Joe about five hours each; they work independently, helping each other only when help is needed. When Joe takes an occasional local job to help pay for costs, however, Pat has to do all of the feeding herself and is exhausted by the end of the day. In fact, Joe says appreciatively, "Pat is the one that keeps this place together."

They also divide other tasks. Pat makes sure all the animals are healthy. She also handles most of the public relations. Joe takes care of repairs, does all of the construction, picks up the food, and conducts tours of the facilities. The facilities need to be cleaned regularly.

The work can be hard, especially during heavy rains or snow and very hot weather. "Depending on the time of year," says Joe, "the chores can be very demanding." In the summer, the animals eat less food but drink more water, which must be kept fresh throughout the day. In the winter, although they have snow to contend with, the Bergerons don't have to cut grass, water trees, water the animals as frequently, or take visitors on tours. But the animals almost double their food intake—the big cats eat a total of three hundred to four hundred pounds of meat per day, and the smaller animals about fifty pounds a day. Joe explains that they need the extra food during cold weather for body conditioning, fat, and warmth.

A typical day for Joe begins with a walk around the property to check on all of the animals. Then he begins feeding the animals and taking care of any maintenance work that needs to be done. When the sanctuary is open to the public, Joe provides a public feeding at two o'clock. This is quite popular; it causes the animals to move about instead of just sleeping, which is a big part of their daily routine. Pat begins her workday by taking care of the indoor animals, a job that she repeats at the end of the day. Then she prepares the food and feeds the rest of the animals in her care, following a carefully planned routine. Baby animals require feeding several times throughout the day. She spreads out her work over the course of the day, taking all day to do it. "Because it's our own place, we can work at our own pace, as long as everything is accomplished at the end of the day," says Pat. "I am able to take breaks when I want to because I'm my own boss." Her routine is much different, however, when she fills in for Joe when he works outside the sanctuary.

Pat and Joe agree that the ideal background for this kind of work is hands-on experience with animals. They once hired a zoologist to assist them. "He knew a lot about animals, but he knew nothing about looking after them," Joe says. Once, when Joe and Pat needed to leave for a few hours, they asked the zoologist to prepare the two o'clock feeding. When they returned, they found him gagging, trying in vain to get the meat ready, his knowledge useless in dealing with this situation. By contrast, one young person who worked at the sanctuary for several summers has gone on to study veterinary medicine. She is now interning at a zoo in Manitoba and will graduate soon. She tells the Bergerons that what she learned during her summers working at the sanctuary was very good training for her work as a veterinarian. Joe is emphatic: "We would hire anyone with hands-on experience over a university degree."

The most essential traits for people wanting to do this type of work are patience and persistence, Pat says. Patience is necessary in dealing with the animals when you need to move them to clean their enclosures or treat them medically. Persistence is important when dealing with the various political problems that those in sanctuary work often face. Pat says that they have been persistent "because the animals are of the utmost importance to us and we'll do whatever it takes within our power to be able to continue working with them." Compassion is also essential in this work. "Sometimes you have to make tough decisions for the welfare of the animals. You have to be certain that the quality of life is all it should be."

Joe agrees that patience is necessary for dealing with both animals and humans. He also emphasizes the importance of common sense—a quality, he notes, that "is not taught in a university or college." It is also important, he says, to "control your emotions, not be afraid, and understand that animals have feelings too." When he is bitten or clawed, Joe blames it on human error—he never blames the animals for the mishap.

Pat suggests that people who are interested in this line of work, especially those who want to open their own sanctuaries, should be financially secure before beginning. Joe simply says, "Don't get into this unless you don't mind being broke all the time, working hard, putting the animals ahead of yourself, and generally not having a life outside of the work." For people who work for someone else at a sanctuary, Pat adds, "Be prepared to work hard and get dirty." But above all, "enjoy the gratitude you get from the animals. It's truly rewarding."

Both Joe and Pat love their work and wouldn't think of any other. What they don't like is dealing with people "who have no clue about animals but are quick to judge."

Joe says that a lot of people initially think they want to do this type of work, believing that it just involves spending time petting the animals, but some volunteers never come back when the work gets hard or don't show up to care for the animals on rainy or cold days. "No one can truly appreciate the work involved in an operation like ours," he says. "The hard work comes first, and then the perks."

Pat and Joe suggest that people who want to get into this type of work should obtain as much hands-on experience as possible. Volunteer work is a good way to get this experience. In addition to giving an edge in getting jobs, experience also lets people know whether sanctuary work is what they really want to do. Small places like the Bergerons' can't afford to hire people to help; the places that are hiring—mostly zoos—require a biology or zoology degree. From their experience, they see some differences between zoo work and sanctuary work. "Animals at bigger zoos are just that: animals," Joe says. "Here they're part of the family."

Although the addition of modern technology, such as computers and faxes, hasn't changed the nature of the work, it does help in gathering information. The Bergerons research carefully before they take on an animal. They read a lot and use email to keep in touch with others who have the same interest. Getting the diets right for a variety of animals also takes research. Pat also notes that having a website gives the sanctuary a lot of exposure.

Joe and Pat are both happy with their work. "The best part is the affection you get from each and every animal," Joe says. "You look after them with no conditions; they respond and allow us to pat and love them up. They're grateful and show us in many different ways that they care for us as much as we for them. Going out in the morning, after all these years, and still seeing the beauty of all the animals is very rewarding." Pat says simply, "I love everything about my work with the animals."

Chapter 10

Caring for Animals

*The greatness of a nation and its moral
progress can be judged by the way its animals
are treated.*

Gandhi

A number of different careers involve caring for animals. The careers
vary considerably in the training required and the percentage of
time actually spent with animals. Veterinarians, for example, are
focused on the health of animals, but they also spend a lot of time dealing with the animals' owners. (James Herriott's popular books about
the life and work of a country veterinarian vividly illustrate how big a
part human owners can play in veterinary work.)

The enormous need for medical care for cats and dogs alone is
shown in statistics produced by the American Pet Products Manufacturers Association for 2000 and 2001. They indicate that in the United
States, there are approximately 68 million owned dogs, and dog owners spend an average of $196 a year on veterinary expenses. As well,
seven out of ten owned dogs were spayed or neutered. Statistics for the
same time period showed 73 million owned cats in the United States,
with their owners spending an average of $104 a year on veterinary
expenses. Eight of ten owned cats were spayed or neutered.

This chapter begins with a description of a variety of careers,
including veterinary technicians and technologists. It also describes
animal behaviorists' work and offers information about holistic and
alternative veterinary therapies: acupressure and acupuncture, basic
and therapeutic nutrition, homeopathy, magnet therapy, massage therapy, and animal chiropractic. Because animals are also used in therapy
for humans, the chapter concludes with some brief information about
work in this field.

VETERINARIAN

Salary Range: Starting about $27,800; average about $63,000; top pay about $82,200.

Educational Requirements: Veterinary degree.

Employment Outlook: The need for veterinarians will remain steady.

Veterinarians care for the health and well-being of animals and, indirectly, for the animals' owners. Their rigorous education and training prepare them to prevent, diagnose, and treat a wide variety of animal health problems. Making a diagnosis often requires doing tests and X-rays using technical medical equipment. Treatment may be anything from setting a fracture or prescribing medication to delivering babies or performing surgery. Veterinarians are responsible for patient care and for the outcome of the care they provide.

In the United States alone, more than half of all veterinarians work in private practice. About half of these practitioners work almost exclusively with small animals; about eleven percent work mainly with large animals: cattle, hogs, sheep, and horses. The remaining percentage have a mixed practice that involves work with both small and large animals.

The field of veterinary medicine has been changing rapidly. Women are increasingly entering the field—the prediction is that by 2005, more than half of the veterinarians in the United States will be women. (In the not-too-distant past, women were not admitted to veterinary schools or were actively discouraged from applying.) There are a number of reasons why women have made such active gains in this professional field. One is that, although veterinarians have a medical degree, their income has not kept pace with that of others in the medical field. Women often tend to choose a career about which they feel passionate, regardless of the salary, whereas men may feel the pressure to earn a larger income in the career they choose, especially if they expect to be the primary income provider for a family. Veterinary work also allows doctors to work on a part-time basis, which means that women can spend more time with their children while working.

Because indications are that women veterinarians are less likely to choose a farm practice, the long-term implications of more women entering the profession may be a shortage of veterinarians for cattle, hogs, and poultry, which reflects a trend in the profession. In the 1940s and '50s, virtually all veterinary work involved farm animals; dogs and cats were treated on the side. Today, however, treating pets makes up about seventy percent of veterinarians' earnings.

Another change in veterinary medicine is the type of patients treated. Although the typical veterinary office still treats mainly cats and dogs, more and more less-conventional pets—lizards, snakes, ferrets, tropical birds—are being brought in for treatment. Veterinary schools have begun to adjust and now offer more courses in treating these species. These courses, in addition to expanding the capabilities of a veterinary office, may lay the basis for veterinary work in a zoo or working in the wild to conserve threatened species of animals.

Other types of work for veterinarians include teaching veterinary students or researching preventative measures and solutions to animal health problems. Such research has contributed directly to finding solutions for many human health problems. Veterinarians also work in research and development for private industry, helping create nutritious animal foods. Veterinarians work in regulatory medicine to control or eradicate animal diseases and protect the public from animal diseases that also affect humans. Public health work, performed by veterinarians for various branches of government, involves controlling diseases and promoting health. Some veterinarians work in the military service in biomedical research and development or other types of research, food hygiene and safety, or treating government-owned animals. A few work in space medicine or wildlife management. Veterinarians may also work in settings as diverse as zoos, aquariums, animal shelters, racetracks, fur ranches, and circuses.

Seven years of university education are required for a veterinary degree. Three of these years are devoted to preveterinary education, four to veterinary medicine itself.

A major reward of a veterinary career is the satisfaction that comes from working in a respected profession that contributes to the health of society. Veterinarians also have the satisfaction of seeing sick animals recover and helping healthy animals stay well. Self-employed private practitioners can set their own hours and work beyond the normal retirement age. Their daily work can be quite varied and interesting. Veterinarians who work for the government, private firms, or colleges usually have pleasant working conditions, regular hours, and a steady income with good retirement programs and fringe benefits.

The disadvantages of veterinary work include long and irregular hours, especially for a new private practitioner. Country vets may work in a variety of settings, sometimes in bad weather. Bookwork, record-keeping, dealing with personnel, and other business matters are also a large part of the operation of a private practice.

See profile on page 194.

VETERINARY TECHNICIAN/TECHNOLOGIST

Salary Range: Starting about $15,000; average $25,000; top pay about $40,000.

Educational Requirements: Technician requires a two- to three-year associate degree; technologist requires a bachelor's degree.

Employment Outlook: Good to above average.

The main difference between a veterinary technician and a technologist is the education required. On the job, both terms are often used interchangeably, although some employers differentiate between the two and have a different level of responsibility for each one. People entering this field should research at a local veterinary office and schools that offer veterinary technology courses before they decide which career to pursue. In this entry, the term "vet tech" is used throughout for both jobs.

The vet tech's role is to assist a veterinarian as a nurse or surgical nurse, laboratory or radiography technician, anesthetist, and client educator. Many vet techs work as supervisors in veterinary practices, zoos, and research institutions. Other potential work settings include pharmaceutical companies, laboratories, kennels, and livestock health management organizations.

Working under the supervision of a veterinarian, the vet tech helps in the prevention, diagnosis, and treatment of animal diseases; performs some laboratory and radiological procedures; prepares animals for and assists in surgery, including monitoring the anesthesia; and gives care before and after the operation. The vet tech also educates owners in the care and nutrition of their animals.

Most vet techs work with domestic animals, but a few work with exotic or endangered species. Although work with endangered species is scarce, it is popular and therefore very competitive.

New graduates of vet tech programs will know how to handle the usual species of animals treated and can perform routine laboratory procedures. They will be familiar with common drugs, veterinary instruments, and equipment. Almost every state has a credentialing exam that vet techs must take and pass before they work in this field. Successful completion of this exam indicates that vet techs have the basic knowledge to perform the duties of their work. Virtually all vet tech positions, however, require additional on-the-job training.

Vet techs may work at veterinary, medical, or dental schools; in hospitals; or for pharmaceutical or biotechnological companies. They usually work as part of an animal health support team. For work that involves assisting in designing experiments, developing new equipment and techniques, and analyzing statistical research data, the vet tech must have knowledge of chemistry, physics, and mathematics.

A vet tech may spend up to fifty percent of the workday in a laboratory, taking and developing X-rays, testing for parasites, examining samples taken from animals, and so on. Those who work in zoos are likely to spend more time outdoors, sometimes researching animals in their native habitat. Collecting precise clinical data is essential in managing zoos; this responsibility usually falls to the vet tech. Vet techs working in animal breeding programs and with exotic animals focus on nutrition in large part. In rural areas, a vet tech may assist a veterinarian in making farm calls to examine pigs, cows, horses, sheep, mules, and chickens, as well as dogs and cats.

A love of animals is essential in this work, as is a desire to help them and ensure their well-being. Other important qualities needed for vet tech work are the ability to take direction well and work both as part of a team and independently.

See profile on page 197.

ANIMAL BEHAVIORIST

Salary Range: $35,000 to $90,000+, depending on the specific work and location.

Educational Requirements: Many have degrees in psychology; other helpful disciplines are biology, ecology, genetics, and zoology. A doctorate is required for college teaching, independent research, and administrative positions.

Employment Outlook: A growing discipline, but currently competitive, with more qualified applicants than positions.

The study of animal behaviors is an old occupation. In early days, people studied the behaviors of animals to make hunting more efficient. In farming societies, they studied animal behaviors to determine how to prevent animals from eating their crops. More recently, people have studied the behaviors of animals they breed or keep as companions.

Animal behaviorists fall into several different categories. Those that observe animals in their natural environments are usually called "ethologists." Those who observe and treat problems with animal behavior (usually pets) in their home environment are "applied animal behaviorists." Other animal behaviorists study animals to understand the neurological and physiological foundations of animal behavior. Recently, animal behaviorists have started to study people and animals living together, as human settlements increasingly encroach on habitats used by wild animals.

Animal behaviorists need to be able to work both independently and as part of a team. Oral and written communication skills are essential, as behaviorists often need to write grant proposals for research, educate the public, and communicate their research results. Good observational skills are also important. Animal behaviorists need to design experiments that are naturalistic and find patterns in the data collected. Vital personal qualities are persistence, patience, and the enjoyment of challenges such as those posed by difficult research problems.

Applied animal behaviorists who work with clients and their pets must be trained to listen closely and objectively to their clients. They need to have a great desire to help, and they must care about the pets and their owners. They must also be able to cope with failure, because not every dog or cat can be changed. These behaviorists work with people just as much as with animals, so they need to have empathy for both pets and the needs and feelings of the owners.

Behaviorist positions that do not require such strong people skills include research, working with zoo animals, or testing animal food preferences. Reverence for life and the ability to accept animal behavior without preconceived ideas are essential qualities for all animal behaviorists.

Where an animal behaviorist works often determines the kind of work they do. Following are descriptions of behaviorist work in several settings.

Universities or Colleges

The largest number of animal behaviorists work in a university or college setting, usually teaching or conducting independent research.

Universities also are increasingly hiring animal behaviorists to use their knowledge to improve the production of livestock, help manage wildlife populations, or provide assistance in controlling pests.

Institutions with large zoology, psychology, or biology departments generally offer the most academic appointments for behaviorists. Some behaviorists work in other departments—such as animal science, anthropology, ecology, entomology, neuroscience, and sociology—and at veterinary or medical colleges. Research into animal behavior increases our knowledge of human physiology and psychology. Research on animals helps in understanding human disease, aging, human learning and intelligence, and the causes of behaviors such as aggression and reproduction. Recent research on animals' brains has contributed to the knowledge of the human central nervous system.

A requirement for working as a teacher or researcher at any college or university is almost always a doctorate. Though a master's degree may be adequate for a few positions, people with a doctorate have an advantage in the job search. This is a growing discipline, and competition for teaching and researching jobs is intense.

Government Agencies and Private Institutions

The number of animal behaviorist positions in government laboratories and business and industry is slowly increasing. Many such jobs involve researching health-related topics, such as the behavioral effects of new drugs or the relationship of behavior and disease. Government agencies in natural resources management sometimes hire animal behaviorists to work in wildlife programs. Environmental consulting companies may need behaviorists to research the effects of changes in habitat on foraging and reproduction in animals.

A doctorate is essential for many of these jobs, and broader training is an aid in getting hired. Some helpful coursework for health-related behaviorist jobs is in physiology, biochemistry, and pharmacology. Experience or training in conservation biology, environmental science, or ecology in relation to populations or communities can be an advantage in obtaining management or consulting jobs.

Zoos, Aquariums, Museums, and Conservation Organizations

Some zoos and aquariums have jobs for animal behaviorists to help in designing healthy habitats. They may conduct research to improve the health and reproduction of animals in captivity or work with field biologists in studying endocrinology, genetics, or nutrition. Some zoos, aquariums, and museums hire researchers to educate the general public about animal behavior using educational displays, tours, and lectures. In museums, behavioral research can be very broad, but it usually includes some aspect of the ecology or natural history of the animals being studied. Conservation groups that hire animal behaviorists are usually involved in areas such as long-term field research, programs to reintroduce species to the wild or to a particular area, or the design of nature preserves. The number of positions for animal behaviorists with conservation groups is limited, but with an increase in the number of these organizations, more such jobs should become available.

Animal behaviorists who work in research or conservation usually need a doctorate in veterinary medicine and broad training in another area of biology, such as animal husbandry, ecology, entomology, herpetology, or ornithology. Educators may be hired with a bachelor's, master's, or doctorate in behavioral or biological sciences. Experience or training in adult or secondary education is desirable for these positions.

Pet Behaviorists Working in Homes

The field for behaviorists who study pets and the relationship between owners and their pets is growing. Animal behaviorists are called upon to solve problems such as house soiling, fearfulness, biting, and growling. The problems are very specific to a particular cat or dog and the environment in which that animal lives (the term "environment" is used here to include the human family and the physical properties of the home).

It is essential that applied behaviorists visit the owners and pets in their home environment when they attempt to diagnose the cause of pet problems. A pet behaviorist needs to have a detailed understanding of the problem and know how the pet and family live, when the problem began, and how the owner has tried to stop the behavior. The behaviorist develops strategies to change the problem behaviors and teaches the pet owner how to use these strategies. Follow-up is an important part of this work.

Some people work full-time as pet behaviorists, but many also conduct applied research and teach. Veterinarians sometimes begin to work as animal behaviorists after discovering that they are skilled at dealing with behavioral disorders. Knowledge of internal veterinary medicine can be a big help in diagnosing behavioral problems in pets.

HOLISTIC MEDICINE / ALTERNATIVE THERAPIES FOR ANIMALS

Salary Range: Varies. Few receive an entire income from one therapy; most practice several therapies or veterinary medicine as well.

Educational Requirements: Currently unregulated. Course-work in specific therapy is needed; most such therapists also have veterinary or massage therapy degrees.

Employment Outlook: As these therapies become accepted, the work will increase, but probably very slowly.

Various alternative treatments and health approaches, usually described under the umbrella term "holistic therapy," are increasingly being used for animals. The term "holistic" implies that the treatments take into account the whole animal and the entirety of the animal's situation. In essence, these therapies treat the animal and not the disease and are often complementary to veterinary care.

Two essential aspects of holistic medicine are prevention and early detection. Holistic practitioners often believe that conventional medicine responds only in an emergency fashion—fixing something that has gone wrong. Important concerns in preventing disease are proper nutrition and a healthy lifestyle. Holistic practitioners sometimes lead the way in diagnosing allergies instead of continuing to prescribe the same medicine for recurrent problems. Holistic medicine may be especially important in providing relief for pets with chronic or incurable diseases.

The various holistic treatments available to animals include acupuncture and acupressure, basic and therapeutic nutrition, homeopathy, magnet therapy, massage therapy, and chiropractic treatments; these are briefly described in the following pages. Some other holistic therapies used for pets are aromatherapy, color therapy, cranio-sacral therapy, and therapeutic touch.

Acupuncture and Acupressure

The use of acupuncture or acupressure is not a substitute for veterinary care but a complement to other treatments. Acupuncture was developed in Asia, and the first recorded use of acupuncture to treat an animal was about three thousand years ago, when it was successfully used to heal an elephant suffering from stomach bloating. It has since been used all over the world and on many different species of animals.

Acupuncture is based on inserting small, sterile needles to stimulate certain points along "meridians" identified by acupuncturists. This stimulation is thought to help enhance the natural healing capacity of the body and restore physical balance to the immune and endocrine systems.

Acupressure uses only pressure to stimulate the meridian points and help balance the energy of the animal. It is a form of touch therapy that can be incorporated into massage or used alone.

Basic and Therapeutic Nutrition

Nutrition is used to help with health problems that may be caused or aggravated by dietary deficiencies or environmental contaminants. Nutritional supplements add vitamins, minerals, and trace elements that may be lacking in an animal's diet or help eliminate toxins or waste from the body. Whereas herbal remedies are often used as preventatives and can also be used to relieve symptoms, nutritional supplements are usually used to help develop or maintain health.

Homeopathy

Homeopathic remedies involve administering greatly diluted amounts of organic substances that are designed to act as a trigger to stimulate the natural immune system of the body. Because stimulating and working with the immune system is a slow process, these remedies may take quite a lot of time to become effective. The remedies aim to treat the patient, not the disease.

Magnet Therapy

The American Medical Association has approved the use of magnets as a treatment for pain, and this therapy is now being used for animals. The beneficial effects claimed for magnet therapy include reduced pain, increased circulation, greater flexibility, and improved sleep.

Massage Therapy

Massage helps reduce pain and discomfort in animals, especially in the case of injuries, arthritis, or hip dysplasia, a crippling joint disease that affects many large dogs. It can help prevent the development of postoperative compensatory tension, increase the rate of healing, and strengthen the immune system. Massage therapy helps improve circulation, relax muscle spasms, enhance muscle tone, increase the range of motion, remove toxins and metabolic waste, and nourish the skin.

Massage is also used for therapeutic relaxation, relieving tension and anxiety. It is useful for horses before races, especially endurance races, and dogs that participate in agility sports or are involved in work that is mentally or physically challenging, such as search-and-rescue, police work, or guiding. It also is beneficial for companion animals. Massage can help animals with a history of abuse or neglect by breaking the association of touch with pain, restoring touch as a source of pleasure, and helping with self-confidence.

See equine massage entry on page 63.

ANIMAL CHIROPRACTOR

Salary Range: Depends on patient visit average, but usually between $30,000 to $200,000.

Educational Requirements: Veterinarian or doctor of chiropractic degree, plus animal chiropractic courses.

Employment Outlook: Increasing, as more people become aware of this field.

Animal chiropractic has only recently been established as a separate and unique profession. There are three designations for animal chiropractic practitioners. An animal chiropractor is a person with a doctor of chiropractic degree and certification from the American Veterinary Chiropractic Association (AVCA), which indicates additional training in the field of animal chiropractic. A veterinarian certified in animal chiropractic has a doctorate in veterinary medicine and certification from AVCA. A third designation, veterinary chiropractor, indicates possession of both a doctor of chiropractic degree and a doctorate in veterinary medicine.

The work of animal chiropractors is similar to that of human chiropractors. They adjust vertebrae, extremity joints, and cranial sutures. Before they work on an animal, the chiropractor obtains a detailed case history from the owner and collects information on previous diagnoses and therapies and the results of any X-rays or laboratory analyses. Before making an adjustment, the chiropractor examines the animal, analyzing posture, gait, and the vertebrae and extremities both in a static position and as gently manipulated by the doctor. Animal chiropractors also make neurological evaluations.

The treatment is based on the case history and examination. After treatment, the chiropractor gives advice on ways to care for the animal—therapeutic exercises and rehabilitation—to ensure the best response to the chiropractic care. Animal chiropractic is not a substitute for traditional veterinary care, and the chiropractor does not dispense medicine or perform surgery.

The AVCA is committed to furthering the profession of animal chiropractic by standardizing the education and conducting research. This professional membership organization provides certification for doctors who have trained in animal chiropractic and works to promote the field to professionals and the public. The AVCA encourages and supports ethically conducted research in this field. It provides advice for AVCA-certified doctors in designing and carrying out research projects, and coordinates this research around the world.

Animal chiropractic is a recent and growing field.

See profile on page 194.

ANIMAL USE IN THERAPY

Animals are often used by therapists in the treatment of humans. The therapeutic benefits of touch and the intimacy that develops between pets and patients are becoming better understood. Animals listen nonjudgmentally to conversations and respond promptly to affection. This kind of unconditional love and acceptance helps many patients in need. Dogs and cats are the most common animals used in therapy.

In cases of aphasia, or brain damage, dogs have been found to aid in the treatment of patients who are struggling to regain speech and coordination. Reaching to pet a dog often seems more pleasant and natural than simply concentrating on lifting an arm to increase range of motion.

Animals have been used in formal psychotherapy for years. The term "pet therapy," in fact, was first coined in 1964 when American child therapist Boris Levinson observed the effect of using his dog in sessions with children who were severely withdrawn. The dog served the role of icebreaker until the therapist gradually established a rapport with the child and could begin therapy. Although interest in the subject predated Levinson's work, he was the first to publicize his findings and sparked research into this phenomenon. Since then, numerous studies have demonstrated the benefits of using pets to increase patients' quality of life in different health-care settings.

Some hospitals have programs where volunteers bring in dogs on a regular basis to help ill children cope with extended hospital stays.

Virginia Commonwealth University Hospitals in Richmond, Virginia, operate Paws for Health, a volunteer program whose purposes are to decrease the children's sense of isolation while in the hospital, give them a nonverbal means of play, and add to their sense of well-being. It follows research showing the benefits of pets in the lives of humans, including reducing stress and anxiety, lowering blood pressure, and aiding in relaxation. The Paws for Health program has strict requirements for both pets and volunteers. The health of both is strictly monitored; participants are carefully screened.

Volunteers also conduct pet visits to some nursing, long-term care, and retirement centers on a regular basis. Cats, dogs, and other small creatures, such as rabbits, are taken to these settings. For residents who love animals, this provides a great deal of therapeutic benefit. Using pets with patients who have autism or dementia often provides unexpected rewards. Additionally, prison inmates and abused children or troubled children who are given responsibility to care for pets have shown increased ability to be rehabilitated and gain valuable communication skills.

Assistance or service animals often help people with physical handicaps. Dogs traditionally have been used in this capacity, but today other animals are being trained to assist people with disabilities, including monkeys, birds, pigs, and even miniature horses. A group known as Helping Hands trains capuchin monkeys to live with and help people with severe disabilities or paralysis. This endeavor uses volunteers extensively in the socialization of the monkeys and students to do the actual training. The Guide Horse Foundation in North Carolina uses volunteers to train miniature horses to perform a seeing-eye function for sight-impaired people. These horses provide assistance for people who are afraid of or are allergic to dogs or who simply have a great love of horses.

RESOURCES

Academy for Veterinary Homeopathy
P.O. Box 9280
Wilmington, DE 19809
phone: 866-652-1590
email: office@theavh.org
www.theavh.org

American Academy of Veterinary Acupuncture
(AAVA)
66 Morris Avenue, Suite 2A
Springfield, NJ 07081
phone: 973-379-1100
fax: 973-379-6507
email: office@aava.org
www.aava.org

American Animal Hospital Association (AAHA)
P.O. Box 150899
Denver, CO 80215-0899
phone: 303-986-2800
fax: 303-986-1700
email: info@aahanet.org
www.aahanet.org

American Association of Bovine Practitioners
P.O. Box 1755
Rome, GA 30162-1755
phone: 706-232-2220
fax: 706-232-2232
email: aabphg@aabp.org
www.aabp.org

American Association of Equine Practitioners
4075 Iron Works Parkway
Lexington, KY 40511
phone: 859-233-0147
fax: 859-233-1968
email: aaepoffice@aaep.org
www.aaep.org

American Association of Zoo Veterinarians
3400 Girard Avenue
Philadelphia, PA 19104-1196
www.aazv.org

Animal Behavior Associates
4994 South Independence Way
Littleton, CO 80123
phone: 303-932-9095
fax: 303-932-2298
email: info@animalbehaviorassociates.com
www.animalbehaviorassociates.com

Animal Behavior Society (ABS)
Indiana University
2611 East 10th Street #170
Bloomington, IN 47408-2603
phone: 812-856-5541
fax: 812-856-5542
email: aboffice@indiana.edu

American College of Veterinary Behaviorists
www.veterinarybehaviorists.org

American Holistic Veterinary Medical Association
2218 Old Emmorton Road
Bel Air, MD 21015
phone: 410-569-0795
fax: 410-569-2346
email: office@ahvma.org
www.ahvma.org

American Society of Animal Science (ASAS)
1111 North Dunlap Avenue
Savoy, IL 61874
phone: 217-356-9050
fax: 217-398-4119
email: asas@assochg.org
www.asas.org

American Veterinary Chiropractic Association
442154 East 140 Road
Bluejacket, OK 74333
phone: 918-784-2231
fax: 918-784-2675
email: amvetchiro@aol.com
www.animalchiropractic.org

American Veterinary Medical Association (AVMA)
1931 North Meacham Road, Suite 100
Schaumburg, IL 60173
phone: 857-925-8070
fax: 847-925-1329
email: avmainfo@avma.org
www.avma.org

Canadian Veterinary Medical Association
339 Booth Street
Ottawa, Ontario
Canada K1R 7K1
phone: 613-236-1162
fax: 613-236-9681
email: info@canadianveterinarians.net
www.cvma-acmv.org

Delta Society
875 124th Avenue NE, Suite 101
Bellevue, WA 98005-2531
phone: 425-226-7357
fax: 425-235-1076
email: info@deltasociety.org
www.deltasociety.org

Guide Horse Foundation
P.O. Box 511
Kittrell, NC 27544
phone: 252-433-4755
email: info@guidehorse.com
www.guidehorse.org

Helping Hands: Monkey Helpers for the Disabled
541 Cambridge Street
Boston, MA 02134
phone: 617-787-4419
www.helpinghandsmonkeys.org

International Association for Equine Dentistry (IAED)
www.iaeqd.org

International Association for Veterinary Homeopathy
(IAVH)
334 Knollwood Lane
Woodstock, GA 30188
phone: 404-516-5954
email: office@iavh.at
www.iavh.at

International Society for Behavioral Ecology (ISBE)
Department of Zoology
The Ohio State University
1735 Neil Avenue
Columbus, OH 43210

International Veterinary Acupuncture Society
P.O. Box 271395
Ft. Collins, CO 80527-1395
phone: 970-266-0666
fax: 970-266-0777
email: office@ivas.org
www.ivas.org

North American Veterinary Technician Association
(NAVTA)
P.O. Box 224
Battle Ground, IN 47920
phone: 765-742-2216
email: navta@navta.net
www.navta.net

SPAY/USA
2261 Broadbridge Avenue
Stratford, CT 06614
phone: 203-377-1116
fax: 203-375-6627
email: spayusawebsite@aol.com
www.spayusa.org

Veterinary Institute for Therapeutic Alternatives
15 Sunset Terrace
Sherman, CT 06784
phone: 860-354-2287

Profile

VETERINARIAN AND CERTIFIED ANIMAL CHIROPRACTOR
Alison Seely

"I have always been obsessively interested in animals," says Dr. Alison Seely, veterinarian and certified animal chiropractor. Because of her allergies to dogs, however, Seely didn't consider veterinary medicine as a career option while in school. "I opted for a career in marine biology, completed a bachelor of science, and then studied nonallergenic seals for my master's thesis," she says. "In the process, I found that I was always more interested in the health of my subjects than in my research questions. I also was being regularly adjusted by my husband, a human chiropractor, and found that my allergies had subsided to a tolerable sniffle instead of full-blown wheezing." So after finishing her master's degree, Seely went to veterinary college.

As a veterinarian, she explains, "I am essentially a medical doctor for animals. I juggle the jobs that are shared by many specialists in human medicine—surgeon, general practitioner, emergency doctor, pediatrician, oncologist, palliative care specialist, and even psychiatrist for behavioral problems." Seely sees a range of animal species as patients, "from the small painted turtle and budgies to Clydesdale horses and Charolais bulls." Each has a different physiology and anatomy.

Having experienced the positive results of her husband's work, Seely decided to train further to become an animal chiropractor. In this role, she explains, "I address the spinal health of my patients. I examine their spines by motion palpitation and adjust vertebrae that are out of alignment." Most of her chiropractic patients are dogs, cats, and horses. They are referred to her for a variety of reasons: "obvious back pain, lameness, disease that has not responded to conventional treatment, and proactive care, particularly for athletes in the animal world."

Seely's career progression is not typical for most veterinarians. She went from marine biologist to becoming a veterinarian treating a traditional mix of animals. After her chiropractic studies, she became a small-animal veterinarian with a large-animal chiropractic component. At present, she works almost exclusively in animal chiropractic for small animals and horses.

Applicants for a four-year veterinary medicine degree need a minimum of three years of undergraduate education, but most applicants have a bachelor of science. An important requirement for veterinary applicants is consistently high grades. "A longer course of undergraduate studies or a degree gives an applicant more options," Seely says, "as higher grades can be submitted and lower grades deleted in preparing the application."

According to Seely, the specialization of animal chiropractic "is offered only to graduates of veterinary or chiropractic colleges. It is completed in six four-day modules over one or two years."

During a normal day when Seely worked full-time as a veterinarian, she would see sick animals, consult with owners about behavioral problems, treat chronic illnesses such as diabetes or cancer, examine and vaccinate healthy animals, check up on hospitalized patients, write reports on their health and progress, and ensure that animals scheduled for elective surgery were healthy. Most of the surgeries were spays and neuters; she also might have performed exploratory surgery, orthopedic procedures, or fracture repair.

Since specializing in chiropractic, Seely now spends only half a day each week practicing regular veterinary medicine. "In my capacity as animal chiropractor," she says, "I divide my time between taking appointments at animal hospitals—I work out of two clinics in two cities—and providing a mobile service to stables within a two-hour radius of my home. I take a history, examine and palpate the patient's spine, and do a gait analysis. I then adjust the patient." Seely generally recommends a reexamination in one to four weeks, depending upon the symptoms, and she sees some patients on a monthly "proactive" basis.

Her work requires a number of special skills and a great deal of knowledge. The ability to memorize and absorb large amounts of information during veterinary training is an essential asset. As both a veterinarian and animal chiropractor, she relies on her knowledge of animal anatomy and physiology. One of the most important personality traits for a career such as hers is empathy with animals. "Surprisingly," she says, "a liking for people is equally essential in the veterinary profession, because the owners are clients and they are who we talk to." She also considers diplomacy very important "because veterinary practices are large, often hierarchical businesses." Verbal and written communication skills are crucial and are used every day. Other vital skills that she cites are palpation sensitivity and an understanding of animal behavior and signals. This last is especially important. "I would be bitten or kicked if I ignored these cues," she says.

In her work, Seely says, "the working conditions in terms of animal contact are marvelous. Other than time with my colleagues or travel time, one hundred percent of my time is with animals. I have a lovely mix of indoor and outdoor work with its inherent pluses or minuses, depending on the weather."

Seely believes that the career of animal chiropractic has a good future. "I am as busy as I choose to be at this time due to the scarcity of trained practitioners." She notes that veterinary journals currently contain many advertisements for veterinarians with alternative skills. She also sees a good future for conventional veterinary medicine, noting that the number of positions advertised every year exceeds the number of available graduates and salaries are becoming more competitive.

In her work, Seely uses both email and the Internet extensively. "I communicate with clients by email," she says, "and often email or fax my notes to other practitioners." Further, she has found that the Internet often replaces textbooks in researching obscure disease processes and helping establish diagnoses. Clients who have Internet access are becoming more educated and focused with their questions, which, she says, "keeps us on our toes."

Her advice to potential veterinarians and animal chiropractors is to get as much exposure to the work as possible. "Volunteer at a vet clinic, work on a farm, and get adjusted by a chiropractor," Seely suggests. "Read about chiropractic philosophy."

Because the cost of setting up a new office can be prohibitive, recent graduates often associate with an existing practice. Seely advises new veterinarians to seek one that has a good reputation, is practicing current medicine, and has senior partners who can serve as mentors. For new animal chiropractors, associating with an existing practice "provides referrals, secretarial support, and the options to use X-ray machines, medications, and so forth."

"Animal chiropractic grows by referral, particularly from satisfied owners," says Seely, but she also does her part to spread the word. She hands out brochures explaining animal chiropractic to her patients' owners, local chiropractors, and veterinary clinics. She gives talks to dog clubs, pony clubs, and 4-H groups—"I rarely turn down an invitation to lecture to my peers or the public," she says. She also volunteers to check dog spines at an annual charity dog walk. Seely is on the editorial board of a veterinary journal written for the public and contributes regularly. "The more exposure animal chiropractic receives," she notes, "the busier all animal chiropractors become."

Seely dislikes only a few aspects of her job. "I dislike euthanizing animals and refuse to euthanize healthy animals or perform declaw or ear-cropping surgeries," she says. "I also dislike the long hours in the car for the mobile animal chiropractic practice."

The things she likes far outweigh the negatives. "I love working with animals on a daily basis," she says with enthusiasm. "It is marvelous to be paid for hugging animals all day! I like being instrumental in restoring health to my patients, both through allopathic [traditional] and chiropractic treatments. The dramatic recoveries I observe after chiropractic adjustments are very gratifying. I also enjoy working with people. In my chiropractic work, particularly, I develop a relationship with both owner and patient through continued frequent visits."

Profile
VETERINARY TECHNICIAN
Lisa Skentelbery

"I think I always knew that this was what I wanted to do," says Lisa Skentelbery, veterinary technician. "I have always loved animals, and I had dogs when I was growing up." She has worked for twenty-six years at a veterinary hospital in Kanata, Ontario. In fact, she got into this career after she worked at the clinic as a sixteen year old. In that job she learned the difference between the work of a veterinarian and a technician, and she realized that the technician's work was the one that interested her.

When Skentelbery describes her work as a veterinary technician she compares it to that of a nurse. (This definition is in line with a name change being considered by Ontario's professional vet tech association, from "veterinary technician" to "veterinary nurse.") "We help care for animals by performing basic husbandry, nursing care, and assisting in the diagnosis and treatment of diseases," she says. "One of the reasons I like my profession is that we do more than most nurses in human medicine—we take and develop X-rays, we do our own labwork, we assist in surgery, and we do obstetrics and postnatal care. Most of this would only be done by specialists on the human side."

Skentelbery says that it is ideal for young people to gain on-site experience before they start vet tech coursework; she wishes that co-op programs had existed when she was in high school. Such experience, preferably in a veterinary setting, ensures that prospective technicians can deal with the sight of blood and animals in pain.

Skentelbery recalls that in the intensive, two-year veterinary technology course she took, "we learned about companion, farm, and laboratory animals and had several of each species to look after on an ongoing basis so that we got used to their daily care—handling and restraining them so that procedures could be performed." Courses such as this one are sometimes taught by correspondence or distance training, but she considers hands-on contact to be extremely important.

On a typical day, the veterinary technician arrives at the hospital early and makes rounds to check on each patient. Skentelbery provides food, water, and medications to each patient as needed. Some animals need to be walked or have their bedding changed. When the patients scheduled for surgery that day arrive, she checks them into the hospital. "Any pre-operative bloodwork or X-rays are taken so that the results can be analyzed by the veterinarians as they arrive. Any special equipment, instruments, or medications are assembled so that we are ready to proceed." In the meantime, work at the hospital continues and she may be asked to help with other appointments or to draw blood from a patient needing diagnostic work.

In surgery, technicians administer anaesthesia to the patients, whether injectable or inhalant anaesthesia or a combination of both. Additionally, Skentelbery says, "in surgery, the tech may assist, donning gown and gloves, or simply monitor the patient and hand the veterinarian instruments as needed. After surgery, the tech stays with the patient while it recovers and lets the vet know if further pain medication seems necessary." The vet tech is, she notes, "the eyes and ears of the vet."

Another important role that techs play is that of public educator, according to Skentelbery. "Often it is the tech who spends extra time with the pet owner, helping them to make decisions about preventative care, nutrition, behavior counseling, and so on." She finds this especially important because of the abuse people can unwittingly put their animals through due to ignorance. The rest of her day may be spent doing labwork and recording results in a patient's history. "Many of the clinical logs in the hospital are maintained by the techs," she notes. "They also ensure that the instruments and equipment are cleaned and sterilized for the following day's use. They constantly check in on the patients to make sure they are resting comfortably."

After working at the hospital for a number of years, Skentelberry has gradually taken on more administrative duties. As the practice manager, she orders drugs, supplies, and therapeutic foods, and she meets with representatives of the various drug companies, obtaining information on new medications to pass on to the veterinarians. She hires, fires, and oversees the staff, carrying out performance reviews for technicians and other staff. She also handles customer service issues. Overall, she enjoys this addition to her veterinary technician duties.

She uses current technology extensively in her work. "In the last decade or so," she says, "we have moved to computerized record-keeping. This has made for much more effective, clear treatment plans and exchange of information between caregivers." The ability to fax records also eases the transfer of records, and she considers email and the Internet valuable tools.

Two important traits for the veterinary nurse are empathy and compassion, and Skentelbery emphasizes that these are needed "not just for the animals, but for their caregivers as well, especially as our society becomes more aware of the importance of the human-animal bond." Other essential knowledge and skills are "attention to detail and an aptitude for math and science."

Skentelbery is very positive about her work: "I like helping—both people and animals," she says. "Nothing makes me happier than seeing someone with a new puppy or kitten that's getting off to a healthy, happy start. I also have had the satisfaction of seeing pets at the end of their lives and being able to help ease their suffering," she adds. "I feel strongly that euthanasia is one last kindness that we can show animals." Although Skentelbery says that her work hours can be long, "for those of us devoted to animal care, it is worth it when you work with a great, compassionate team."

The advice that Skentelbery has for persons interested in her career is this: "Get some practical experience and make sure that this is what you want to do and are suited to do. Be prepared to work very hard, and sometimes thanklessly, to learn your trade. Always be professional and empathetic in your care of animals. Research the courses offered and find one with lots of hands-on training included."

The field of veterinary technology is growing, Skentelbery says, with veterinary technicians receiving more recognition as important members of the veterinary healthcare team. She says, "The demand now exists for valued, skilled, professional technicians to join veterinary practices. Just put yourself out there and find a team that fits!"

Chapter 11

Some Job-Search Tips

The greater the number of job-hunting
avenues you use, the greater the likelihood
that you will find a job.

Richard Nelson Bolles,
What Color Is Your Parachute?

Now that you've reached this chapter you've probably focused on a specific career or type of work. If you are ready to begin looking for a job, it will be helpful to do some additional research before you concentrate on your job search. Look at books and other resources that cover the particular career in greater detail. Especially valuable, if you have no work or volunteer experience in your chosen field, are informational interviews with people currently working in the field. This will help round out your knowledge of that type of work and will also give you contacts that may be helpful when you begin your job search.

This chapter explains how the Internet can help you, reviews some of the critical aspects of this part of the job-search process, and points the way to additional and more detailed information.

THE INTERNET

If you haven't already used the Internet in your search for career information, you may want to start now. If you're not familiar with it, get some assistance from local sources, such as a library or career center. You might also consult the Resources section at the end of this chapter.

A cautionary note, however, before you spend any time using the Internet in your career search: As you may already know, it is easy to become engrossed in an Internet search, following links from one site to another. Before you begin each Internet session, decide how much time you will spend online and how much information you want to locate. This will help ensure that your time is well spent.

The Internet contains a wide variety of resources, whose usefulness varies as widely as do the books in a bookstore. Before you dip too deeply into any specific Web site, try to evaluate the site and its purpose. Use the same criteria you use when you open a printed book. Determine who established the site and why, and then decide how these factors might affect the validity of the information. Also try to find out when the information was posted; you want to use the most current information in your search.

The Resources section of each chapter in this book contains the web addresses of the various organizations listed, whenever available. This is a good place to begin, especially if you're not Internet-savvy. Many of these organizational websites contain career information and actual job listings, or links to sites that have this information. As you would expect, sites vary considerably in the type and amount of information they contain.

Some companies and organizations advertise jobs on the Internet and accept resumes for these jobs online. Governments throughout the United States, especially at the national and state levels, also list available jobs, as do Canadian national and provincial governments. Many universities and colleges list jobs on websites, but these are often protected from use by individuals other than their own graduates. You should explore all assistance available from your own institution, while also checking other sources.

You may also decide to establish your own homepage, complete with your resume. Some individuals have found work using this method. Other websites allow you to post your resume without charge. Additionally, some discussion groups on the Internet give job listings. Used wisely, the Internet can be a wonderful tool for finding a good job. In fact, recruiters are increasingly going online. Of some forty-three hundred recruiters surveyed in 1998, 37 percent used the Internet, a 10 percent increase from the year before.

If you wish to use the Internet extensively in your job search, be sure to check the Career Crossroads Web site (and other books and sites) in the Resources listing at the end of this chapter.

WRITING YOUR RESUME

A resume is an essential job-search tool, and preparing one is among the first steps to take in a job search. Remember that a resume is a selective summary of your skills, abilities, work, and study experiences. It is not a life history, but it should provide enough critical information about your background to interest a potential employer in interviewing you.

Writing your own resume, instead of hiring a resume service to prepare one for you, is a valuable part of the job-search process. Although resume writing takes effort, it is well worth your time and is excellent preparation for the focus on your background that will occur in the job interview. If you do consult an outside source for help, be sure that you are actively involved in the process.

In writing a resume, be certain to include all of your applicable skills and experience to ensure that you are presenting yourself as favorably as possible. Because a resume is usually the second representation of yourself to a potential employer (after your cover letter), it must be clear, concise, and well-written. Before you begin to write the actual resume, take some time to jot down information that you think should be included. Organize your information under headings such as the following:

Career Objective

Your career objective, a simple statement of the kind of career you are seeking, should also include brief information about your skills or background. Some people do not feel comfortable writing a career objective and prefer to give a skills summary. The value of this information, however, is that it helps focus your resume and immediately gives a potential employer a good overview of your background.

Skills and Work Experience

Write out your work experience and then elaborate, listing the skills you used in each job. It is important to describe what you actually did or accomplished. If you are a recent graduate or are changing careers, you can include summer, part-time, or volunteer positions as well as extracurricular activities. The focus here should not be on any job title, which can often be misleading, but on the job content. What actual skills did the job entail?

Your resume should show the skills you have used and give examples of your accomplishments. In detailing your skills and accomplishments, use action verbs. If you're having trouble finding the best action verb, consult one of the many available resume books. They usually give comprehensive listings of such verbs.

If you are changing careers, remember that you may use some of the same skills in the new career that you used in previous work. For example, you may be moving from a supervisory position to an editing and writing position; many supervisory positions involve writing and editing, and they also require good organizational and decision-making skills—which are certainly necessary for editing and writing jobs.

Education

Give your educational background, listing any degrees and your major or concentration. You may also want to list some major courses and/or your thesis title. If you don't have a great deal of work experience in the field, this information may be especially important.

Awards and Honors

List any awards, special recognition, or honors you have received. On the actual resume you may include all of these or be selective, listing only those specifically related to your chosen field of work or those showing significant achievement.

Interests and Hobbies

Sometimes interests and hobbies have a direct bearing on your career goals and should be included in a resume. They also help round out your presentation of yourself and give prospective employers a more complete idea of your background. But don't use these to the exclusion of information that may be more directly career-related.

After writing out this information, you may want to check with close friends and family members to see if you have left out anything of importance. Getting the perspective of others who know you well can be quite helpful in working through this somewhat tedious aspect of resume writing.

When you're actually writing the resume, keep in mind that it is essential to use correct spelling and grammar. It's wise to consult a few of the many excellent resume books available when you begin writing your final draft. There you can find many samples of different types of resumes. The Resources section at the end of the chapter includes some recommended books. Many of the job-search books listed at the end of chapter 1 also have helpful resume sections.

Remember that there is no one correct way to write a resume; every employer has different preferences. But these general principles should guide you through resume preparation. Additionally, you must feel comfortable with the end product; your resume is about your unique skills and experiences, so use content and a format that presents the unique person you are to best advantage.

Increasingly, resumes are being submitted online through a website or sent by email. Additionally, computers are now being used to read resumes by scanning them for keywords; you must therefore be certain that your resume contains the keywords that are important for the type of work you seek (and which, of course, are part of your background). In fact, including a keyword or key phrase may be the factor that will land you an interview.

Types of Resumes

The two basic resume types are functional and chronological. The chronological resume organizes work and educational experiences in reverse chronological order (beginning with the most recent and working backward). The standard format lists each employer and job title plus a brief description of the job content. This is most commonly used by people changing positions in the same field.

The functional resume emphasizes skills and the content or function of previous jobs, volunteer work, or personal experience. This type of resume is usually used by those who are changing careers and want to emphasize skills they have gained. Employers often do not like functional resumes, because they can obscure work history.

If you like the idea of emphasizing skills and past accomplishments, you could consider using a functional format that includes past employment, usually called a modified functional resume. The advantage of this type of resume is that the focus is squarely where it should be—on your demonstrated skills.

COVER LETTERS

Always include a cover letter with any resume, whether you are responding to a job advertisement or sending a mailing to many potential employers. A cover letter must be written in correct business style with no grammatical errors and must be produced by typewriter or word processor—never handwritten.

The purpose of a cover letter is to interest an employer in reading your resume, so it must be interesting and to the point. It must also explain why you're sending your resume—for example, in response to a job ad, because the organization was recommended to you by someone (give the name if it is a person of influence), or because you are looking for work in this field. If the letter is in response to an advertised job, focus on the particular skills and experience you have that relate to this job.

The first paragraph of the cover letter should explain your purpose in sending the resume. The main body of the letter should briefly describe you and how your unique skills and abilities could fill the employer's needs. Be specific in explaining how you have used your skills to accomplish a certain goal. The closing paragraph should lead to action. You may wish to give a time when you will get back in touch rather than saying that you look forward to hearing from the employer. You could also state your willingness to send more information.

CREATIVE JOB SEARCHING

It is essential to use creativity in your job search and employ many strategies. Apply for jobs listed in newspapers and in association or trade publications, but don't let these be the sole focus of your job search. Also approach personal contacts you may have from summer, volunteer, or part-time jobs.

To expand or develop a network of contacts, conduct informational interviews; these can yield information about a career in addition to contacts in the field. The purpose of an informational interview at this stage of your job search is to ask for advice or suggestions on your job-search strategy. To arrange for an interview, contact someone who is in the career that interests you. Tell this person that you would like some suggestions on your job-search strategy, and ask for a few minutes of his or her time. Bring a list of questions to the interview and conduct yourself very professionally. Ask for names of other people in this field whom you could also contact for helpful information.

Don't ask for a job in this interview, but be prepared with a resume in case one is requested or a job possibility is mentioned. After the interview, send a letter of thanks, including a resume, if you haven't already left one. You may want to contact these people later in your job search to let them know that you are now looking for a job in the field.

In addition to good job-search information, this strategy yields good contacts in the field. If these contacts were impressed with you during the interview, they may be glad to help you when you let them know you're actively searching for a job. A recommendation from individuals already in this field can be invaluable, because most managers place more faith in the word of people they know than in the actual hiring process.

Through these contacts, you may hear of positions before they are advertised, when there is less competition. Informational interviews will also help you become more comfortable in interview situations; this can yield dividends when you interview for jobs later on.

In addition to consciously working to establish a network by conducting informational interviews, you may locate job possibilities by using the network you already have. Speak with family members, friends, professors, and contacts from part-time, summer, or volunteer work.

Joining the appropriate association and attending its workshops and conferences is another way to network, gain contacts in the field, and learn about job possibilities. Jobs are often listed in association newsletters or journals.

Another strategy for finding jobs is to mail resumes to carefully selected employers. Target organizations or companies that have the type of positions you are seeking, and send your resume to the appropriate supervisor, not to personnel. Research to obtain this person's name; it's better to direct your resume to an individual than to a title. Some directories have this information, or the switchboard operator of the company may be able to give you the name. These carefully targeted mailings can lead to interviews, to more networking possibilities, and to actual jobs.

THE JOB INTERVIEW

Many people find the job interview quite frightening. Good preparation should help make this important step in the job-search process much less intimidating. It's also helpful to keep in mind the purpose of the job interview, which is basically for the candidate and the employer to assess each other and decide if this is a good job fit. You probably were invited for an interview because your "paper trail"— your letter and resume—seemed to fit the qualifications the employer had in mind for this position. Employers interview to make certain a candidate's professional background and work experience match the job that is available. They also want to assess your personality and decide whether you will fit in with the company.

As you prepare for a job interview, try to learn as much as you can about the department in which the opening exists, including its responsibilities and functions. Also try to learn about the work culture of the potential employer (for example, is it rigidly hierarchical with all decisions and initiatives coming from the top, or is there room for individual initiative? In which type can you work best?) and the personality of the person who would be your supervisor.

This research will help you be more relaxed as you go into the interview. It will also help you formulate questions to obtain more information about the company, evaluate it, and decide whether you want to work for it. Additionally, your knowledge of the employer will be evident in the questions you ask during the interview. The interviewer will be impressed by your research as an indication of your initiative and your desire to work for his or her company.

Before the interview, review your skills and be ready to give specific examples of ways they could benefit the employer. Be prepared for open-ended questions such as, "Tell me about yourself." The employer is not looking for your life history but for pertinent information about you that is related to the job in question. Most job-search books include lists of the types of questions generally asked in interviews. It's good to check these out and formulate answers for each one in preparation for the interview.

Don't worry if you're nervous. As you have more interviews, you will become more comfortable with this aspect of job seeking. Besides, if you are too relaxed, you may not do your best in the interview. Practicing with a friend before the interview can help calm you and prepare you for formulating your thoughts on the spot.

So prepare well, learn all you can about the employer ahead of time, and review the skills and accomplishments that you will stress in the interview. Then go and do your best. Know realistically that you will not be offered all jobs for which you interview, and likely you will discover that not all of these jobs or employers are quite what you were looking for, either. In addition, competition is keen for many jobs, and many qualified people may have applied. Don't think that not being offered a job reflects negatively on you. Work to maintain your self-confidence during your job search, which may last longer than you anticipate.

Reading about interviews in some of the many books on the market can be helpful as you prepare—but don't build interviewing up to be more difficult than it really is. There is no one right way to interview; as with a resume, each employer is looking for different things, so what will impress one person won't impress another. You can only do your very best to represent who you are when you go to an interview.

A FINAL WORD

As you go about finding a job, possibly the best advice is to use more than one strategy. Don't use the Internet to the exclusion of all other methods, for example. And don't neglect the strategy of sending out mass mailings to potential employers. The virtue of these mailings is that the sheer number of letters sent will help you identify employers that have appropriate job openings. The success of this type of job-search campaign is based on a high volume of letters sent. The average response to such a mailing is 2 to 3 percent, so if you mail fewer than 100 letters, you may feel your campaign was a failure.

A mass mailing can be an expensive proposition, but if it yields a job it may be worth the cost. In 1998 the National Business Employment Weekly reported on a mass mail campaign in which some twelve hundred letters were mailed out. Within a short period of time twenty-one responses expressing interest were received; eventually three job offers resulted.

If you do decide to send a mass mailing, design it thoughtfully. Carefully target potential employers and aim your letter and resumes to the types of needs these employers would have. Remember to obtain the name of the supervisor in the area where you want to work. This is a lot of work, and it will demand commitment on your part—but it can pay off handsomely.

RESOURCES
Internet

Bolles, Richard Nelson. *Job Hunting on the Internet, 3rd ed.* Berkeley, Calif.: Ten Speed Press, 2001.

Crispin, Gerry, and Mark Mehler. *Careerxroads 2004: The Directory to the Best Job, Resume, and Career Management Sites on the World Wide Web.* Kendall Park, N.J.: MMC Group, 2004. (See also http://careerxroads.com/.)

Dikel, Margaret Riley, and Frances E. Roehm. *Guide to Internet Job Searching, 2004–2005 ed.* Chicago: VGM Career Books, 2004.

Gabler, Laura R., ed. *Career Exploration on the Internet: A Student's Guide to More than 500 Web Sites.* Chicago: Ferguson Publishing Company, 2000.

Krannich, Ron, and Caryl Krannich. *America's Top Internet Job Sites, 2nd ed.* Manassas, Va.: Impact Publications, 2003.
Nemnich, Mary B., and Fred Edmund Jandt. *Cyberspace Resume Kit 2001: How to Build and Launch an Online Resume.* Indianapolis: JIST Works, 2000.
Weddle, Peter D. *WEDDLE's 2004 Job Seeker's Guide to Employment Web Sites.* Stamford, CT, WEDDLE's, 2004.

Resume Books
Enelow, Wendy S. *Best Keywords for Resumes, Cover Letters, and Interviews: Powerful Communication Tools for Success.* Manassas, Va.: Impact Publications, 2003.
Jackson, Tom. *The Perfect Resume: Today's Ultimate Job Search Tool.* N.Y.: Random House Inc., Broadway Books, 2004.
Kennedy, Joyce Lain. *Resumes for Dummies, 4th ed.* Hoboken, N.J.: John Wiley & Sons Limited, 2002.
Krannich, Ronald L., and William J. Banis. *High Impact Resumes and Letters: How to Communicate Your Qualifications to Employers, 8th ed.* Manassas, Va.: Impact Publications, 2003.
Noble, David F. *Gallery of Best Resumes: A Collection of Professional Resumes by Professional Resume Writers, 3rd ed.* Indianapolis, Inc., JIST Works, 2004.
Weddle, Peter D. *Weddle's InfoNotes (WIN) Writing a Great Resume: The Fastest Way to Winning the Job You Want.* Stamford, CT, WEDDLE's, 2002.

Resume Websites
Job Smart Resume Guide (http://www.jobstar.org/tools/resume/index.cfm).
What Color Is Your Parachute?, electronic edition (http://www.job-huntersbible.com/).

Cover Letters
Kennedy, Joyce Lain. *Cover Letters for Dummies, 2nd ed.* N.Y.: IDG Books Worldwide, 2000.
Krannich, Ron, and Caryl Krannich. *Nail the Cover Letter: Great Tips for Creating Dynamite Letters.* Manassas, Va.: Impact Publications, 2005.
(See under Resumes for additional cover letter books.)

Interviews

Enelow, Wendy S. *KeyWords to Nail Your Job Interview: What to Say to Win Your Dream Job*. Manassas, Va.: Impact Publications, 2004.

Kennedy, Joyce Lain. *Job Interviews for Dummies, 2nd ed.* N.Y.: Wiley Publishing Inc., 2000.

Krannich, Ronald L., and Caryl Rae Krannich. *Interview for Success: A Practical Guide to Increasing Job Interviews, Offers, and Salaries, 8th ed.* Manassas, Va.: Impact Publications, 2002.

——. *Job Hunting Tips for People with Not-So-Hot Backgrounds: 101 Smart Tips That Can Change Your Life*. Manassas, Va.: Impact Publications, 2005.

——. *Nail the Job Interview: 101 Dynamite Answers to Interview Questions, 5th ed.* Manassas, Va.: Impact Publications, 2003.

——. *Savvy Interviewing: The Nonverbal Advantage*. Manassas, Va.: Impact Publications, 2000.

General Job-Search Books

Krannich, Ron, and Caryl Krannich. *201 Dynamic Job Search Letters, 5th ed.: Writing Right for Today's New Job Market*. Manassas, Va.: Impact Publications, 2005.

Occupational Outlook Handbook 2004–2005. Washington, D.C.: Superintendent of Documents, 2004. Available on the Internet at: http://www.bls.gov/oco/home.htm.

Stoodley, Martha. *Informational Interviewing: How to Tap Your Hidden Job Market, 2d ed.* Chicago: Ferguson Publishing Company, 1997.

The Canadian Job Directory. Toronto, Canada: Sento Media Inc., updated annually.

See also the Resources section in chapter 1. Many of those books give information about all aspects of the job search.

Index